SHADOWS OF THE ANCESTORS

SHADOWS OF THE ANCESTORS

A play in three acts

ONYECHI MBAMALI

authorHOUSE®

AuthorHouse™ UK Ltd.
1663 Liberty Drive
Bloomington, IN 47403 USA
www.authorhouse.co.uk
Phone: 0800.197.4150

First published in November 2009.

Published by AuthorHouse   11/21/2013

ISBN: 978-1-4678-8045-9 (sc)
ISBN: 978-1-4678-8046-6 (e)

Shadows of the Ancestors

Dedicated to

● **Chukwudifu** ● **Afoma** ● **Monso**

(Children of God)

CAST

Ifediba . . . . Crown Prince of Umudimkpa
Apiti
Ebili   } Ifediba's companions
Okpijo
Chime
Igwe . . . . the late king
Oyidi'a
Mmikiaku   } the king's wives
Akwamma
Akaeze
Dikeogu
Ebekuo   } the high chiefs
Mmanko
Eto'odike
Orimili
Ajofia
Ugochi . . . . Princess of Umuachala
Ajachi . . . . .her slave girl
Ibenibe . . . . Ajachi's father
Nwamgbeke . . . . Ajachi's mother
Okafor . . . . Ifediba's valet
Ude
Echezo   } citizens
Ikuku
Anyandimmuo . . . . diviner
Otondo . . . . head slave
Anizoba . . . . captive
2 palace guards
2 male attendants
2 maids
Dance troupe

ACT 1, SCENE 1

*Open space on the way to the Umudimkpa palace at nightfall.
Two men meet.*

Chime: The drums of the square are yet to speak. Still no news from
the watch?

Ude: The drums of the land will speak no more. Umudimkpa is
like a drum without the drummer.

Chime: I hate this suspense. Someone should talk if what we hear
is true. Why do you elders eat silence as food? Why not just
announce the news if the old man is dead?

Ude: Kings do not die: they join their ancestors.

Chime: That is a fable to keep the women-folk and infants in the
back quarters. This drama is not fooling anybody. It is clear
to everybody now that the great one is dead. You elders
should advise the palace to announce it.

Ude: You talk like the youth that you are or a stranger that you
are not. The demise of the king of Umudimkpa is not a
song for the open market place. By parable it is whispered
mouth-to-ear to freeborn sons of the land. That is the
custom. Umudimkpa is still a land of warriors.

Chime: If the land must go by tradition, it is bad time for the slaves.
I hear it takes a hundred heads to pad a royal grave.

Ude: More, I fear. I was a small boy when the Igwe's father joined
          his ancestors. What my eyes saw would appall a mad butcher.
          But the Sky-king changed all that by his Great Reforms. No
          human sacrifice has happened in the last seven years.

Chime: And Ajofia the High Priest has opposed like a wounded
          lion. If that man had his way, everybody would be slave and
          every slave a headless body. Do you think he could muster
          support now to reverse the king?

Ude: I fear that Ajofia has more support than the high noon might
          have revealed. It is the dark night that brings forth evil
          beasts. Umudimkpa is passing through its darkest night.

Chime: You sound just like my father. Why does your age prefer
          to see shadows in the brightest sun? Umudimkpa has no
          better dawn than what is about to happen. The Crown
          Prince, Ifediba is my age. In a matter of days, he will sit
          on the throne. Youth will reign and Umudimkpa will see
          the difference. My generation will breathe a new life into
          the withered scrubland, purge this kingdom of the filth of
          morbid customs and the stench of decadent traditions. A
          sweet fragrance will cover this land, a song in every heart, a
          smile on every face. You elders are the past of sorrows; we
          are the future of confidence.

                                        [Enter Echezo]

Echezo: What past does he know and what future is he bragging
          about?

Ude: Let him be, Echezo. It is the arrogance of youth which puts
          urine in the water pot.

Echezo: If it doesn't break the water pot straight away. Friends, the
          omens are not good. If Ifediba does not arrive by dawn, the
          future may be a mass grave in the forest.

Ude: Why do you say that?

Echezo: Ajofia the High Priest. He is putting so much pressure on the Prime Minister. Tonight the Council of High Chiefs must decide on the way forward. Ajofia will attend.

Chime: Ajofia coming to the palace?

Ude: The palace he shunned for seven years?

Echezo: After seven years of defiant absence, he mocks the palace tonight with a demand for blood sacrifice.

Chima: But Akaeze should resist that.

Echezo: How long can anyone resist Ajofia's group when the Crown Prince is not here to mount the throne? Two weeks have passed. Every day brings close the dreaded massacre.

Chime: Ifediba will come back.

Ude: Why delay for even a day?

Chima: Are you sure he got the correct message? These old people can play terrible games in mischief.

Echezo: Custom does not dribble the wise. Your friend received the empty snuff box of his father two weeks ago. Since then, three sets of emissaries have been sent to him in the forest of Isibuke.

Chime: What is he supposed to do with his father's snuff box?

Echezo: It is the signal that his hunting days are over. He must return home to give the empty stool of his father the warmth of his royal buttocks. That is the custom, but where is the man?

Ude: His father was the true Sky-king. His reign was a drumbeat to which the whole earth danced.

Echezo: That dance may end tonight. If Ajofia and his cohorts take over, the kingdom will be red again with the running blood of slaughter. All because of one young man who is lacking in understanding and cannot be advised.

[Lights dim. Announcer's gong off-stage]

Announcer *[off-stage]*: By the mouth of the king. By the mouth of Igwe, the Sky-King, the one who towers above the hills and mountains, who slays a man on the day his life is sweetest, whose countless eyes outnumber the apertures of an anthill . . . to the six clans of Umudimkpa, the land of warriors . . . to every free-born adult male who sprouts from a rooted family tree . . . take count of all the strangers in our midst, all the captives of war too, and all other persons as are numbered amongst your possessions . . . take count of one and all . . . and ensure they are well . . . ensure they are well . . . By the order of the king, the palace so announces. By the jaws of the king, Igwe, the Sky-king whose rage is fiercer than the wrath of thunder . . .

[Lights fade]

ACT 1, SCENE 2

The stage is dark, deserted. Same night. A twelve-year old lad bursts in, running, falling.

Anizoba *[desperately]*: Somebody save me! Save me, somebody! I am not a slave! I am not a slave!

> *[He runs off-stage. Enter Chime, curious, agitated]*

Chime *[to nobody]*: Who is that? Who goes there?

> *[Enter Ikuku from the opposite direction]*

Ikuku: A free-born in a free land.

Chime: Ha, Ikuku, the strong wind. You are of the guild on the watch, who is the screamer you were chasing?

Ikuku: I saw no one and no one saw me. I am heading to my father's compound. If I were you, I would do the same.

Chime: If everyone goes to his father's house, where is a meeting place? Talk to me, friend. What is new in the palace?

Ikuku: Ajofia will tell you when he meets you.
> *[Exit Ikuku]*

Chime: Ajofia! He is on every lip tonight, like an evil chill. So much dread at the mention of one name.
> *[Voices within]*

1st male voice: Where is that he-goat?

2nd male voice: I think he went this way. Yes, this way!

1st male voice: Stop that slave of the wastelands!

2nd male voice: Don't let him escape!

[Re-enter Anizoba, running, falling]

Anizoba: Please save me! Spare me! I am not a slave! I am not a slave!

[Crouches before Chime. Enter Ude]

Chime: Who are you?

Anizoba: I am a prince of the Ubulu Kingdom.

Chime: One of the ten captives from the punitive raid, last week?

Anizoba: Yes.

Ude: Why are you running then?

Anizoba: We heard the town crier, then they came to take us away. They claim it is for our safety, but I heard them whispering about evil forest. Please help me, good people. I know what happens in the evil forest.

Chime: Nobody will kill you. This is Umudimkpa.

Ude: And there are two Evil Forests, a place and a man. Escape the place, you fall to the man and that is worse for you.

Anizoba: Please save me from both. I am a prince and not a slave.

[Voices within]

1st male voice: Which way have you gone?

2nd male voice: Right over here, mate. I can hear voices. Where is Otondo?

1st male voice: Otondo! Otondo!!

Otondo *[within, panting]*: I am coming! I am not young like you.

> *[Anizoba shifts back and forth in fear, crouches behind Ude]*

Anizoba: Please, good people. Don't let them take me.

> *[Enter Otondo and 2 palace guards]*

Otondo: There you are, Anizoba. I warned you there is no escape for a slave in this kingdom.

Anizoba: I am not a slave. I am a prince of the Ubulu Kingdom.

1st Palace Guard: In this place, you are nothing. Do you hear that?

Anizoba: Please don't let them take me! Good people.

> *[Otondo goes forward, prostrates at Ude's feet]*

Otondo: Owners and sparers of my life. My forehead cleans the ground at your feet. *[He rises, then squats]* I have orders to gather my fellows. The boy behind you is one of us.

Anizoba: I told you I am not a slave. I am a prince.

Otondo: *[Still squatting]*: He is one of the captives from last week—the youngest and the most difficult. Keep him here, he runs there; hold him that way, he runs this way.

> *[Guards move to encircle Anizoba stroking their cudgels].*

1st Palace Guard: Grab him, mate. Let's get out of here.

Anizoba: Stay away from me! People, please don't let them get me.

[Anizoba flits from Chime to Ude as the guards maneuver. Otondo and the two guards corner him and with a rope, tie his hands behind his back]

Anizoba: [*Sobbing*]: Who will speak for me in this place? Who will speak out for me? I am not a slave.

Otondo: I told you there is no escape.

[Otondo and guards shove and drag the struggling Anizoba. A cudgel falls in the struggle as they exit]

Chime: What a tragedy to be prince and slave in one life!

Ude: Every man is both.

Chime: I hate to think so, but you know what? You are right!

[2nd guard returns to retrieve his fallen cudgel]

Chime: Friend, where are you taking that fellow?

2nd Palace Guard *[hesitates]*: If by way of response, you get yourself a dog's head, what will you do with the jawbone?

[Exit the guard]

Chime: Everyone is talking like a masquerade tonight.

Ude: It is a night for masquerades. A wise man must go home.

Chime: Are you afraid of masquerades? Are we not initiates?

Ude: What I sense this very moment is worse than fear. It is a strange chill in my bones. As if an unseen thing is sneaking under my loin cloth.

[Ude covers his crotch with both hands. Chime instinctively follows suit as a clanging bell resounds in the distance]

Chime: It is an Evil Masquerade!

Ude: It must be Ajofia!

Chime: He is heading this way.

Ude: Yes. And he has filled the air with an evil essence. I sense it strongly. See you at dawn.

[Exit Ude. Chime hesitates, Lights dim. Clanging bell is louder. Eerie voice off-stage intones esoterics. Occasionally a bull-horn blares]

Staff bearer   *[off-stage]:*
          Ayii . . . ayiiii . . . . dei, dei, dei
          Dei, dei, dei . . . ayiii
          Night belongs to the initiate
          Tell the laity to flee like fowl
          Wait-and-see will kill the ape
          Tomorrow is upwine for tortoise alone
          Ayii, dei, dei, dei . . . .

[Exit Chime—Staff bearer rushes onto stage, prancing and prowling, simulating the maneuvers of a hunter or warrior. He is thinly loin-clothed, fierce-looking, the heavy bell on the back of his animal-skin apron jangling with every step. From time to time, he drives into the ground his metal staff, a shoulder-high twin-headed rattling spear festooned with white, red and black cloth strips]

Staff bearer   *[on-stage]:*
          The weak-hearted faints at a hint of blood.
          The warrior steeps himself in it, matchet dripping fresh;
          Ayii . . . dei, dei, dei, dei!
          Twice the wood gong invokes the valiant
          First call in life, next call at death
          The pepper shrub is meant to be compassed

There is no art to climb its native stem
Ayii . . . dei, dei, dei

[Enter bull-horn man]

Bull-horn: Ajofia, Evil Forest
Night is your bride
Naked before you
Ambush does not scare a leopard
Summits cannot faze a monkey

*[Blows on the bull-horn as the staff bearer lunges at unseen things
in all directions. Enter Ajofia, rearward first, horsetail in hand, a
palm frond firmly clenched between his teeth. He is dressed in red, a
sleeveless knee-high jumpa over a short loin-cloth.]*

Staff bearer: Tell the defiant bird that shuns the soil.
That perching on the hill, he is still on land.
The raging flame that mocks a brimming pot.
Invites sudden death upon itself

[Bull-horn is blown]

Bull-horn: Ajofia, Evil Forest
Oil bean that breaks curfew at will
Two turtles contend upstream
Tonight will prove which one is male

[Blows the horn]

Staff bearer: Seven years of life missed us sore
Seven calls of time have met us sure
Ayii . . . dei, dei, dei, dei

[Lights dim. Exeunt]

A𝗖T 1, S𝗖ENE 3

Throne room at Umudimkpa palace, same night. [Five chiefs are seated on high stools forming a half-moon. The fourth and seventh stools are vacant]

Dikeogu: It is fourteen days, fellow high chiefs. Fourteen days after the Great One turned his back. Yet the journey to his ancestors he cannot commence. The slaves are strutting as if they own the land; the Crown Prince is nowhere, nowhere to be seen.

Mmanko: It is abomination.

Ebekuo: I still say, leave the slaves out of this matter.

Orimili: The slaves are nothing. Our problem is the Crown Prince. He has the whole kingdom on a string like the wobbly dance of chicken and cloth-line. Excuse me awhile to confer with Akaeze.

[Exit Orimili]

Dikeogu: Fourteen days ... what can block Ifediba's ear so completely that he does not hear the call of duty or show us any respect, emissary after emissary?

Ebekuo: Ajofia will join us tonight. It is good he has accepted to come. Our eyes shall be complete to inspect this crawling thing that has confronted us—whether it is snake or python.

Dikeogu: Has it ever been heard that a prince held up the day of his ancestors? It is clear the gods are pointing to something. Even the deaf could hear the noise of battle.

11

Mmanko: Dikeogu has spoken my mind.

Ebekuo: It is surely an evil knot that has been tied. But this very night we untie it . . . Sport or spell, no power can defy the seven high chiefs of Umudimkpa when we agree on a matter and bang our staffs of office together.

Dikeogu: We did not bang our staffs when the gods prayed us to stand like warriors. I told Igwe to his face that custom is a sacred trust above all of us mortals, that the ways of our ancestors must not be put aside at will. The gods know the difference between the bleating of goats and the blood of human sacrifice. We grew sentimental on slaves and the kingdom has become soft like a suckling baby.

Mmanko: Dikeogu has spoken my mind.

Ebekuo: I do not see how the abolition of a bloody custom makes us soft. We do more exploits in battle now than ever before. Umudimkpa is still the land of warriors.

[Re-enter Orimili]

Orimili: We are the scourge of enemies. From the swamps and forests to the distant wastelands, no kingdom can make "fim" when Umudimkpa roars in battle. The silence of thunder does not imply that it is finished in the sky. What Utarazi witnessed years back, Ubulu has suffered just a few days ago. When our vassals get foolish and forget who we are, we show them the vicious side of our matchets. Umudimkpa is never late to battle. That we no longer behead slaves for rituals is not weakness. It is strength.

Dikeogu: I do not have your coveted eloquence, Orimili—Endless River that Follows His Own Course—but there are times when great words do not amount to great truths.

Mmanko: Dikeogu has spoken my mind.

Dikeogu: How can there be strength when we've been rendered powerless over our own slaves? I cannot in my own compound chop off a few slave heads to release or appease the forces that move with me? I, Dikeogu, Valiant in The Thick Of Battle, whose matchet has plucked more heads in battle than the East Wind shakes down udala fruits.

Ebekuo: I am a warrior like you. So is Eto'odike here. We know like you that the gods of war must drink instant blood. But Umudimkpa has chosen to separate peace from war. At home, we offer the gods the blood of animals; at battle fronts the blood of enemies.

Orimili: The gods seem quite content with the menu. Don't you agree, Eto'odike?

Eto'odike *[stammering]*: W-we ... We w-w-win all-all-all our ... our ... b-b-battles!

Orimili: Our unrivalled prosperity is an open dance. In harvest, in trade, in well-being and enlargement of our families, we see the hand of the gods.

Dikeogu: So why are we in the present mess? *[Silence ...]*
Prosperity may dance. But there is the deceptive gyration of a maiden—it lures a presumptuous warrior to sudden destruction. As Ajofia would say, a man who rejoices that the gods are dancing around him may be celebrating his own funeral.

Mmanko: Dikeogu has spoken my mind.

Ebekuo *[irritably]:* What is in your mind that Dikeogu is always speaking?

Mmanko: Ebekuo! Contain yourself!

Ebekuo: Tell me what Dikeogu said. The gods are dancing at your funeral?

Mmanko: Mind your tongue! Ebekuo! Or it will be your own funeral.

Ebekuo: You dare not threaten me, Mmanko. You dare not even begin . . . .

Orimili: Fellow High Chiefs, fellow High Chiefs: This is not a night to squabble like women.

[Enter Akaeze]

Akaeze: And what is the name of this?

[All rise]

All: Akaeze! Right Hand of Majesty.

[Akaeze takes the centre seat. Others then sit]

Akaeze: Our fathers say that courage is common soil in Umudimkpa, but wisdom is seasonal like rainfall. We need an uncommon rain of wisdom this awkward moment and the showers must commence here. Tonight, we deliberate on the future of our nation. Before long, Ajofia the High Priest will join us. First time in seven years, this revered council will be complete again. We must talk tonight, head or heart; but let our spoken words remember we are the gods—the gods that human eyes can see. That is what Igwe, the Sky-king always advised from that waiting throne. We are the visible gods. By our decisions in this chamber, tomorrow may be farmland or graveyard.

Orimili *[Rising up]:*
Akaeze, Right Hand of Majesty. You have spoken well. I know the sense of duty in this chamber. Even when there are differences in thought, we are always united by the love for the fatherland and the respect for the throne. I know I speak for all of us, Akaeze?

14

Akaeze: Orimili.

Orimili: Ebekuodike, Great Warrior Ever Responsive to Invocations

Ebekuo: Orimili.

Orimili: Mmanko, Sharp Machete That Slays in One Cut.

Mmanko: Orimili.

Orimili: Dikeogu—Valiant in the Very Thick of Battle.

Dikeogu: Orimili.

Orimili: Eto'odike—Effectual Praise of the Warrior

Eto'odike: Orimili.

Orimili: The greatest privilege on earth is a seat in this circle. Every one of us deserves his place. Akaeze will lead.

Akaeze: Thank you, Orimili, but I will not say much until we are complete. Tonight the seven staffs must stamp the earth in one accord.

Dikeogu: It has been a long wait.

Mmanko: Too long!

Orimili: The more stress is this endless wait for the Crown Prince. If he arrives this moment, all is still well.

Ebekuo: We are waiting because we choose to wait for him. What if we commenced the funeral without him?

Dikeogu: Like shaving a man's head in his absence?

Orimili: Until Ifediba sets foot on the palace grounds, nothing can happen. The burial and coronation ceremonies are one.

Dikeogu: I was a stripling lad when the Sky-king mounted his father's throne. I remember the glory of his return from the forest of Isibuke: the frenzy when he was sighted in the distance, the eruption of drums in this palace . . . He danced the prowl of "Ogbuagu", Killer of Leopards. Then, he cut off the heads of three random slaves, letting them roll in the dust. It was a glorious spectacle, just like the thrill of battle.

Mmanko: I was there too. I saw it there. At the king's square.

Dikeogu: I see it afresh, like this very moment. The hailing throng trooping after him to the palace gate. He raises his bloodied matchet to the sky and casts it to the ground before the waiting chiefs. He hands his spear to Akaeze, in evidence that hunting is over. Akaeze places on his shoulders the leopard skin of his ancestors . . . and the cannons boom as we the chiefs escort him into the palace grounds.

Mmanko: That is the custom.

Dikeogu: Yes, the sacred path of our fore-fathers. Why do we permit a change that turns life upside down?

Ebekuo: Life without change is graveyard.

Dikeogu: More often, change is a provocation of the gods.

Mmanko: Dikeogu . . . that is true!

Ebekuo: There is no going back to needless killing. Hundreds of rams are lined up for Ifediba. He may behead as many as he cares.

[A burst of drumming—loud, louder. Voices within, Great excitement.]

Mmanko: The drums!

Ebekuo: *[Excitedly]*: the drums! The very drums!

[*All on their feet*]

Orimili: He is here! Hoa! Hoa! The prowling lion is home to his father's den.

[*Three palace attendants come running in, kneel in one corner, awaiting instructions*]

Akaeze: I thank the gods this terrible wait is over. I will first pour libation to our ancestors. Prepare the women-folk. Light up the palace grounds. Now we may laugh with wide-open mouths.

Dikeogu: It is a great night. Relief has come at last.

Akaeze: Never again will there be human sacrifice in Umudimkpa. We all swore to the Sky-king and we must stand firm on that oath.

Dikeogu: I never swore that oath—everyone here knows. But what I want is the good of our fatherland. The tethered lizard is overdue for release. Let us proceed with the ceremonies.

[*Abruptly the drumming stops. General surprise*]

Ebekuo: Hey, why did they stop? Who asked them to stop?

Akaeze: Exactly what is going on?

Dikeogu: The drumming never stops. This is a bad omen.

Akaeze: I say, who asked them to stop?

[*Exeunt all. Lights dim*]

ACT 1, SCENE 4

Throne room at Umudimkpa palace, same night. The three aging queens stand dejectedly in the corner. Orimili, Ebekuo, Dikeogu, Eto'odike and Mmanko are seated.

Ebekuo: Confusion! Unpardonable confusion.

Dikeogu: Abomination he calls confusion.

Mmanko: It is abomination

Ebekuo: How could they do such a brainless thing? Do they eat food through the nose?

Eto'odike: I-I-I w-wonder!

Dikeogu: The gods are pointing at something we are not seeing.

Mmanko: Very true!

Ebekuo: Some mistakes are just not tolerable.

Dikeogu: I am worried. Indeed very deeply worried. How can Ogbuagu drums play except for the Crown Prince?

Orimili: It is a blunder. They sighted Ajofia and mistook him for the Crown Prince.

Dikeogu: Those drums are sacred. They speak the mind of the gods.

Oimili: They speak only to welcome the king from the rare travel.

Dikeogu: Now they've played for Ajofia, a man who has not stepped a foot in this palace for seven years. Aren't the gods telling us something?

[Enter Akaeze, brusquely shoos off the three old queens]

Akazue: Mothers cannot avoid blame for the failings of their children. See what Ifediba your son is doing to king and kingdom.

Akwamma: The whole affair is not natural. I say it is not bare-handed, Akaeze; do look at it with the knowing eyes of an elder. Witchcraft is what they have cast on my beloved son so he wouldn't know what he is doing. It is witchcraft, Akaeze—vile and vicious witchcraft.

[Exeunt the three queens]

Akaeze: It is only a consenting lizard that a waiting serpent may swallow. The Crown Prince of Umudimkpa is a fortress of the gods—impregnable to witchcraft, divination or enchantment.

Orimili: That is true, Akaeze but only when Umudimkpa stands in one accord—and the seven staffs of high office are lifted around the throne. When our seven staffs stamp the earth in one voice, as we hope to do tonight, the warrior spirit of our ancestors shakes the heavens and torments our foes.

[Enter Ajofia rear-first. He looks formidable with palmfrond strip clenched between his teeth and white chalk line encircling his right eye.]

Ebekuo: Ajofia is here!

Mmanko: The Evil Forest himself!

Dikeogu: Dread of the Ancients!

Ebekuo: Untrodden Groves of Darkness!

[Ajofia faces the empty throne, removes the palm frond strip from between his teeth, mutters awhile, walks over to the wall and leans his staff with the six others]

Ajofia: Mortal or spirit, let every being receive his due. Ajofia has one question only: Is Umudimkpa now ready to appease the deities?

Orimili: Ajofia, I welcome you on behalf of Akaeze and the council of high chiefs. Your stool is waiting like a bride.

Ajofia: The gods forbid I join in wasting words. Did you not hear the Ogbuagu drums? Who were they playing for? Where is the man who should sit on that throne? What manner of high chiefs are we who relish talking without seeking answers to simple questions? A man whose thatch is on fire does not sit down to a friendly chat.

Orimili: What exactly does Ajofia want?

Ajofia: It is not Ajofia but what the gods decreed—even before you and I were born. Seventy heads to cleanse the land this very night. Seventy more at sunrise to commence the rites.

[Silence, Orimili is about to speak. Akaeze waves him down and stands up]

Akaeze: Ajofia may speak for the groves and shrines. Akaeze will speak for the throne. "Seventy heads" is a small matter for Umudimkpa. Our warriors can reap that number and more, from any field of battle. But not a drop of human blood shall be shed in this land under my watch.

Ajofia: Ajofia refuses to be provoked like seven years past. But the gods of my fathers will not be mocked in my life time. Who

20

dares to serve Agbala and Ogwugwu with cold flesh as fed to vultures? What is sacrifice to the gods of war without the shriek of oblation and the instant blood? Only confirmed fools would bait the gods and not become their preferred sacrifice. Ajofia calls for a vote of the staffs.

[There are all-round gasps and expressions of surprise.]

Dikeogu *[Rising]*: Have we already come to that?

Orimili: By custom, only Akaeze calls for a vote.

Ajofia: Are we still under custom? Haven't we turned the whole world upside down?

[Ajofia strides to the wall and grabs his staff]

Akaeze: Akaeze will overlook the slight to his office. The peace of the kingdom is more important than the privilege of any stool. I am the one who invited Ajofia to rejoin this council. Let Ajofia go ahead and call for a vote.

Ajofia: Ajofia will appease mortals but only after the gods. Fine me if you may and I will pay anything in kolanuts or cowries, pots of wine and oil, wraps of cloth or tubers of yam, labour or even lands. Ajofia is not fighting the throne—only defending the path of our ancestors, lest the land dies and we perish from the earth.

Mmanko: That is my very mind!

Ajofia *[Raising his staff]*: Seventy slave heads this very night?

[He stamps the floor with the staff and waits. Mmanko walks over and takes up his own staff]

Mmanko *[Stamping the staff on the floor]*: Seventy slave heads! Dikeogu .. ?

Dikeogu: You all know where I stand on this matter. But I do not think we should rush a vote of staffs before the vacant throne.

Ebekuo: What we resolved is to enquire of the gods which course to run, why the canoe is drifting and the paddle in our hands is speaking a strange language.

Akaeze: That is why you were invited, Ajofia!

Ajofia: So, you now want to consult the oracles? Pray, what would you hear from them that Ajofia has not told you again and again? Seventy slave heads to appease the angry gods.

[Stamps the staff on the floor.]

Mmanko: Seventy slave heads!

[stamps the staff on the floor]

Ebekuo: I say, let the oracles direct.

Ajofia: Even the oracles tremble before the powers of this ancient throne. You will not find a diviner to dare the firewalls that garrison the throne of Umudimkpa. Only one man in this whole world can attempt it . . .

Orimili: That is Anyandimmuo of Umolum. We all know that.

Ajofia: It is a journey of three days from Umolum, and Anyandimmuo is now blind with age, frail. It is not possible to bring him here.

Akaeze: Akaeze has something to say about that.

[Akaeze rises, takes a few steps away from the others]

Anyandimuo is right here with us. He is waiting in the guest room. Since this afternoon when he arrived, he has refused to do anything unless the seven high chiefs are present and consenting. That is why I sent for you, Ajofia. Let every man take his place and be quiet before the oracles.

[Lights dim. Fade]

ACT 1, SCENE 5

Throne room at Umudimkpa palace. The high chiefs are all seated. Anyandimmuo divines, seated on a mat, an earthenware pot draped with white cloth before him. He casts cowries, peeps, mutters

Anyandimmuo: It is still a mere void. I don't understand it. The gods are not speaking . . . .

> *[He casts the cowries again and again.]*

Still nothing, no word . . .
Owners of the land, if anyone here is opposed to this enquiry, I will go back to Umolum. I came as a friend of Umudimkpa. The Sky-king was my pal for life . . . I don't understand this blockade.

Akaeze: We all are behind you, Anyandimmuo, Eye of the Spirits. Come, fellow high chiefs. Let a vote of the staffs reaffirm our support.

> *[The chiefs take up their staffs and ring the throne]*

Akaeze: Do we object to this divination or do we say yeah?

All: We say yeah as one,
My staff of office says yeah.
As one, we say yeah!

> *[All stamp the floor]*

Akaeze: Once is enough for the truth. Thrice is best for assurance.

[All stamp thrice and remain standing. Anyandimmuo resumes
ministrations]

Anyandimmuo: Hear my mortal invocations
All you whom I serve, all you who serve me
Which way has the python climbed up
It now refuses to climb down?
Where is the eye of the ant
In the fury of the hurricane?
The fires have razed the scrubland
The cactus must tell the tale of the wilderness.
Tell me what to say, ye immortals

[He casts the cowries: All watch]

Silence is stress in ambushment
But what is the boast of thunder
If lightning would not travel?
Are they not twins in the womb of the skies?
Darkness is a cloak but Night is naked
The brilliance of fire is a plucking from the sun.
Right or wrong: election is the heart's
A penitent ear would still hear rotten deeds
Tell me what to say, ye immortals

[He casts the cowries, peeps, mutters. Lights dim. Fade.]

ACT 1, SCENE 6

Ifediba's camp in the forest of Isibuke, earlier that evening. Three youngsters are lazing around. Enter the middle-aged Okafor.

Apiti: He doesn't want to be disturbed. That's final!

Okafor: I don't require anybody's permission to enter his presence. Keeping an eye on him is my birthright, and all through his sojourn here, it is a special duty. By custom, I am his shadow.

Apiti: Custom. A man declares what he wants to do with his own life and you speak of custom. What is custom? The path of the weak and sick.

Ebili: Custom can be so boring.

Okpijo: It is like getting down with an old woman. There is no thrill, no adventure. Tell me, Okafor. Have you ever done a woman of your mother's age?

Okafor: When you get home, ask your mother.

[Okpijo drops his calabash and charges forward. Apiti deftly restrains him.]

Apiti: Chill, my friend. Every woman is fair game and that includes my own mother. The only problem in life is when we take anything too serious. Like the way Okafor wearies himself with custom.

Okpijo: Advise him to keep his custom to himself. This age does not need it.

Apiti: Ifediba will tell him by himself as always. Let's step aside as usual and just keep within earshot. Custom may have his little say; we are the boys; we get our way!

[Okpijo, truculent, picks up his calabash]

Okafor: Apiti, they call you, The Slippery Soil that Brings Down the Unwary. You imagine that you are up where nobody can match you. But we shall see in the end. You will never escape the coming wrath. Mischief cannot go unpunished for ever.

Apiti: Okafor, my senior, your homilies are so predictable, and so boring. The Crown Prince will tell you better as always. Ha! Ha!

[Exeunt Apiti, Okpijo and Ebili]

[Okafor bends, passing under the cross-bar of the check-point in front of Ifediba's hut. He claps his hands to announce his presence and calls out to the unseen occupant of the hut]

Okafor: Ogbuagu, Killer of Leopards, I greet you . . .

[repeats the clap in the ensuing silence]

Okafor: It is I, Okafor, Rear Watch of the Throne and Life Escort of Royalty.

Ifediba *[within]*: Leave me alone, Okafor. I have no wish to see any old man.

Okafor: Custom forbids I leave you alone. Duty demands that I talk to you. Give me audience, Ogbuagu. Salt and oil can never boycott each other.

[Ifediba emerges from the hut. Tall, elegant, arrogant]

Ifediba: Why don't you just chill? I mean—just leave me alone. I know what I am doing. I can take care of myself!

Okafor: A king is not allowed to worry about himself. That is my duty, the reason I exist.

Ifediba: Your idea of duty is torture to my spirit. See, nothing you say will ever change my mind. I will not leave this place without the woman I love.

Okafor: That woman is trouble

Ifediba: Leave that to me to worry about.

Okafor: You are king.

Ifediba: I have my life to live.

Okafor: What can I say to make you understand there is a big problem? See, you can have any woman you want.

Ifediba: Except the one I want.

Okafor: She is not fit for you . . . . You are the King of Umudimkpa! That woman is a common . . . . .

Ifediba: Shut up your mouth!

Okafor: I did not mean to insult her. But I must call the truth by name. I am the elder here, the one to blame if a she-goat is left on tether whilst in labour pains.

Ifediba: That is the sickening hypocrisy I find in you elders. You can worry about a tethered goat but you cannot feel the pain of a pregnant woman. How do you think Ajachi would survive if she hears that I've left her to her fate and run back to my country? That woman loves me with every nerve in her body . . .

Okafor: Every woman would love the Crown Prince of Umudimkpa.

Ifediba: Ajachi is special. And . . . she is pregnant for me!

Okafor: That pregnancy is an entrapment. If you accept paternity, it is an open affront to the great princess of Umuachala whom you are expected to marry.

Ifediba: I am resolved to follow my heart and be true to myself. I do not love Ugochi, Princess of Umuachala. I love her slave girl Ajachi and I will take her to Umudimkpa if that is the last thing I do with my life.

Okafor: Ugochi will kill that woman. Unlike us, Umuachala is not kind to slaves. She is free to do anything to her . . . and she will.

Ifediba: I am not blind to what I have to do. For two weeks now, Ugochi and I have been playing fox and rabbit games. She will not win. I shall.

Okafor: You have the snuff box of your fathers, Ogbuagu. Umudimkpa is counting the days. It has never been so.

Ifediba: Stop worrying your bald head.

Okafor: Duty is sacred, Ogbuagu.

Ifediba: The duty of custom is blindness. My sense of duty is a lamp of love. In my kingdom, no one will be slave.

Okafor *[aside]:* That woman is an evil potion brewing to wreck the world.

Ifediba: What did you say?

Okafor: I said—uh . . . may you increase in wisdom.

[Re-enter Apiti]

29

Apiti: Hot news from a runner! Hottest news! Guess who is coming this way.

[Trades knuckles with Ifediba in youthful camaraderie]

Ifediba: Who?

Apiti: Who but the princess, Ugochi!

Okafor: Princess Ugochi herself?

Apiti: Live and direct!

[Trades knuckles with Ifediba]

Ifediba: All these days, she wouldn't talk. Now she comes on her own, even to my camp. I didn't even invite her.

Apiti: My tactics can never fail. Trust me always, Ogbuagu. I have the brains to deliver the rains. When she sent word that you should come to her festival dance, all these people said you should go. Okafor here was almost going to strangle me. But I told you to ignore her. Is she not a woman? Surprise and suspense are your best weapons, or you cannot tame women. I know how they think. It is three days into the festival. Now she comes on her own, like a fly to the spider's net.

Okafor: Ogbuagu, please hear me. This is not a sport of insects. It is the fate of two great kingdoms. That young lady is a symbol of her people's pride. You have hurt her badly already. I have no idea where all this is leading to. Please treat her with respect.

Ifediba *[pensively]*: I have heard you .... Leave me alone, for now. Both of you really.

[Okafor and Apiti hesitate, size each other up. Exeunt, Apiti first,
then Okafor. Fade]

ACT 1, SCENE 7

Ifediba's camp in the Isibuke forest, very late evening. Ifediba is seated on a rock—alone, head-bowed, empty drinking gourd in hand. He raises the gourd. A male attendant rushes in with a calabash, kneels at his feet, pours palm wine. At Ifediba's signal, he drops the calabash and exits.

[Enter Ugochi, elegant and haughty, a fly-whisk in hand.]

Ifediba: The Princess of Umuachala dignifies our hunting grounds.

Ugochi: Isibuke forest is shared ground for two kingdoms.

Ifediba: Only one has the hunting rights. You meet the Chief Hunter.

Ugochi: There was one in the legends, the sorry fellow who went messing around with female antelopes, in defiance of the gods. He brought home leprosy.

Ifediba: Is that what you bring with you?

Ugochi: No, sunflower. I bring with me a bleeding heart, the wrathful pangs of rejected affection. You have trampled in the dust my pride as a woman. I'm only here to ask why I deserve this from you.

[Ifediba pats a space on the rock by his side]

Ifediba: Come, honey pot. Sit down . . . Sit down.

[Ugochi is reluctant. Ifediba goes to her]

Ugochi: No, please. Don't touch me.

[She sits. Ifediba paces, then follows]

Ifediba: You are class, Ugochi, a true princess.

Ugochi: In your mouth, that sounds like an accusation . . . This must be a bad dream. You are a Crown Prince. How could you mess up with a common slave girl?

Ifediba: I thought we've gone beyond these demonstrations.

Ugochi: We've gone beyond nothing! I don't even know what I am doing here, talking to you. You make my skin crawl.

Ifediba: Well, that's unfortunate.

Ugochi: *[after a long pause]*: Look. You and I are supposed to marry, no?

Ifediba: It is an expectation, yes. People expect it.

Ugochi: You led me on. You made it look like we were heading there. What am I supposed to think now? Could it be that all that time you walked in my shadows, popping up at odd moments, hanging out everywhere I turned, it wasn't me you needed? You were trailing my personal attendant, a slave girl? And I was sending her to you all the time . . . You must have thought me very stupid . . . Both of you . . . You laughed behind my back, didn't you?

Ifediba: This kind of talk does not help.

Ugochi: Help what?

Ifediba: Move things forward.

Ugochi: I'm not sure what you want to move forward. Can you imagine what I've just found out? That girl is . . . pregnant. *[A pause]* I don't suppose that surprises you.

[Ifediba rises, moves away]

Ifediba: I don't know what you are hinting at. Ajachi is your girl. I always told you I'm fond of her.

Ugochi: It is more than fondness, but I was so blind and trusting. The early warning came in whispers, but I dismissed it all as baseless gossip. Fond of her, he says. Can you swear to a truth? Swear by the gods of your fathers that the child in her womb is not yours.

Ifediba: The gods of my fathers require no such oath!

Ugochi: Then just answer me direct: is that child yours or not?

Ifediba: Why do I need to answer such a rude question?

Ugochi: Because if you don't, I'll believe what I already assumed. Then, the child and its mother shall die.

[They glower at each other]

Umuachala is not Umudimkpa. The festival ends tomorrow. Then they die, mother and child.

[Fade]

33

ACT 1, SCENE 8

Ifediba's camp in the forest of Isibuke, the night deepening.
Okafor paces. Others are seated on the ground around a camp fire.

Apiti: Brains, I tell you. Brains! Superior tactics will always win.

Ifediba: Ebili, move the waves. It's a night of nerves. The plot is too
            tight. Since I gave assent to it, I've become captive to fear.

                        [Ebili pours palm wine from a calabash]

Ebili: A strong head breaks the gridlock, even the clamp of steel.
            The head is not strong if the calabash remains full.

Ifediba: Pour me the torrents. I feel like drinking a tide tonight.

Ebili: A brimming tide would sink sorrows
            And drown the lonesome tears
            The waves I pour would wash away
            Worries and death fears
            So sing to the night, O calabash, sing to the moon and stars
            For mouths open we swim in you or dawn would come too late

Ifediba: Nothing must go wrong, Apiti.

Apiti: You have my guarantee, Highness. It's all about brains.

Ifediba: Nothing must go wrong.

Apiti: Relax, Your Highness. Trust me.

Ifediba: It is not their killing slaves that worries me, but how they do it.
            The brutality has no limit. Everyone invents his own cruelty.

Apiti: They are my grand-mother's people. I know how they think.
            Their envy of Umudimkpa is making them mad.

Ebili: I will make a wicked song for them.
            Remove from my feet a thorn of grief
            This thorn of grief
            This thorn of grief
            I go no more to Umuachala.
            A turn of grief
            A turn of grief

Apiti: They can never match us, so they out-do themselves in
            folly and wickedness. Cruelty is courage, and savagery is
            strength.

Ifediba: The look on Ugochi's face this evening. You should have
            seen that! When she swore that mother and child shall die,
            I realized that these people are not human beings. I have
            taken a final decision. Let tomorrow happen today.

Okafor: Umudimkpa and Umuachala are two powerful neighbours.
            We enjoy with them a tradition of mutual respect, a history
            of peace. It has been so from the beginning.

Ifediba: Things shall be different from now on. Never again shall
            anyone be killed because he is slave. In fact, nobody shall be
            called slave anymore all through the lands.

Okafor: Ogbuagu, Umudimkpa does not make laws for Umuachala.

Apiti: That was true yesterday; but things are different, starting
            tonight. The laws can be made from only one source. It all
            depends on you, Highness.

Okafor: Please don't listen to such deceptive counsel, Ogbuagu. The peace of generations rests only on respect for common boundaries. So it is between us and Umuachala.

Apiti: He is talking of peace. Your Highness, if you don't search beneath the ordinary meaning of words, you can never know what these old people are hiding.

Ebili: Or what they are pushing.

Apiti: True, my brother, true. What is peace but cowardice if we continue to allow Umuachala to butcher men, women and children in the name of slave? Your Highness, it all depends on you. The armies of Umudimkpa shall move at your command. There is no peace without conquest.

Okafor: The gods forbid your evil machinations. Umudimkpa will never fight their in-laws and brothers . . .

[Ifediba raises a fist, halting further words]

Ifediba: My in-laws and brothers are people who will not slaughter fellow human beings in the peace of private homes. I repeat, there shall be no more slavery in these parts. My kingdom shall provide freedom and justice to all, and human life shall be sacred. Anyone who cannot see himself in that light should not bother to return with me to Umudimkpa . . .

Okafor: Ogbuagu will not banish his subject. Umudimkpa is fatherland for ever.

[The wood gong, ekwe sounds in the distance]

Ebili: *[Intermittent with the ekwe notes]*:

             I hear your message, *ekwe.*
             I hear you clear, wood messenger of the braves.
             I hear the hoof beats of antelopes

The delicate chuckle behind your throaty laughter
Now you make broadcast to the seven hills
Tell the wilderness of the ripened palm fruits
Tell me more, tell me more
About the stampede and the fearless storm
Which leg of cockroach? Any survival tale?
The lake may be sleeping, the iguana is about

[The melodious dance notes of Agbogommuo masquerade floats in and gets louder]

Apiti: I have the brains, Your Highness. Superior tactics. See, we simply took advantage of their dance festival. It worked as I told you.

Ifediba: I just want to see her face, hold her in my arms again.

Apiti: I promised and I've delivered

[Enter a dance troupe in resplendent costumes, escorting three masquerades. They dance in circles]

Okafor: This is a violation of custom. Masquerades are not allowed in Ogbuagu's presence after sunset.

Apiti: Your time is past, old man. Can't you get that? The world is moving on.

[One of the masquerades stays back as the rest are led away by the troupe head]

Okafor: This is unacceptable. It is wrong!

[Apiti confers with Ifediba]

Apiti: Your Highness, she's all yours. She may go into your hut and change.

Masquerade: That won't be necessary.

[The masquerade unmasks itself. It is Ajachi.]

Okafor: The gods of my ancestors!

Ifediba: Ajachi, my treasure . . .

[Ifediba and Ajachi embrace. She proceeds to remove the costume]

Ajachi: Are you sure you understand what you've begun? You have stepped on the lion's tail. The forest will never be the same again.

Ifediba: My eyes are wide open. I take full responsibility.

Okafor: With due respect, Ogbuagu, I cannot keep silence at this abomination. A king is above sentiments and emotions. What is happening here in your presence is a desecration of our customs. A woman robed as masquerade! Abomination!

Ajachi: My prince, you can see why you need only progressives around you. That's what Apiti says so often and I think he is right. We must talk about that later. Let's get about. Time is not our friend.

Ifediba: Of course, my treasure. What are you all gawking at? Move everybody. Mobilize immediately. We go this night. Back to the fatherland.

[Frenzied excitement. Ifediba takes Ajachi into his hut. Exeunt all. Fade]

ACT 1, SCENE 9

Ifediba's camp in the forest, deep in the night.
Ebili is alone, leaning on a tree in the half-light of the dying
camp fire. There is a voice-over as he plays his flute, his
calabash of wine hanging on a rope slung over his shoulder

Ebili: Some will take an age to pack belongings
Some will pack belongings to wreck an age
Ebili is different, light as a feather
I belong to my calabash, she will go with me
She's a faithful bride, my flute is witness
I am Ebili, child of deepwaters
I pot the waves, I pour torrents
Music on my flute, the notes of running brooks
Uniting noon and night in wedlock of no sorrows

[Enter Ajachi. She goes to a corner, sits on a stone]

Ages after us, who will remember this night?
And what name shall be called in our memorial?
A cast of courage, a flock of folly?
Murmurs of midnight encourage my fear of boldness
If the unsheathed knife betrays the warrior
Whose coffin comes first is a guess for lunatics
First step presumptuous, the next precarious
Makes stampede the only dance of elephants
The pathway of the leopard never lacks a tale
The deaf need no warning of a battle ahead

Play your flute, Ebili, pot more waves
Unleash strongest tides of wine-song in up-wine
Drown these nagging thoughts, these stubborn
    props and promptings —
    echoes of yesterday
The debris of apprehension and relics of fear
Let us do this journey, let us go
A canoe that taunts a paddle is not wise
Let the lake forget what she swallowed
The swimmer braces for a date with destiny
A vacant hut is humming on the other side.

[Enter Ifediba]

Ifediba: I still can't find the snuff box. Ajachi, my treasure.

[Ajachi is sulking]

Ajachi: What is all the fuss about an ordinary snuff box?

Ifediba: You don't understand. This snuff box is special.

[Exit Ebili]

Ajachi: I will never understand a snuff box so special it counts more to you than a moment with me. You even brought that Okafor who treats me like a leper. Snuff box! Snuff box! as if the sky was about to fall. I know when I'm not wanted; so I left you both to snuff and box all you care. I came out here for fresh air. The flute was playing a lovely tune, even though it made me sad.

Ifediba: Treasure mine, the important thing is that we now have each other. You and I shall be together for the rest of our life. Nothing and nobody will ever make you sad again.

[Ajachi eludes his embrace]

40

Ajachi: No, prince, I've been reconsidering this whole thing.

Ifediba: And what does that mean?

Ajachi: Seriously, we cannot do it, my prince. I cannot go with you to your country.

Ifediba: Where is this kind of talk from? What is wrong with you?

Ajachi: It is wake-up time. For me, at least. See, my prince, it has been a wonderful feeling—like walking on air . . . dreaming I could be queen . . . in Umudimkpa of all places! But sleep is over. I am wide awake. I am a slave girl; you are king. The gods in their wisdom shaped our paths to be separate. Go to your throne, my prince. My place is here.

Ifediba: What about my baby?

Ajachi: He lives in my womb as you live in my heart. If I live, he will one day know about you.

Ifediba: Ajachi, listen to me

Ajachi: No, you listen, my prince. I am not good for you.

Ifediba: Let me be the one to worry about that.

Ajachi: The world would never let you forget.

Ifediba: If you love me as I love you, we can face the world together.

Ajachi: It is not as easy as the words, my prince. The strongest love will lose its green if every day is harmattan.

Ifediba: My love for you has no season. It is the unending rush of a waterfall, the eternal blossom of the wild pumpkin. This love can never fade.

41

Ajachi: Your people would never forgive me. They would say I charmed you.

Ifediba: If that is said, is it untrue?

Ajachi: Please be serious, my prince.

Ifediba: I am dead serious.

Ajachi: This is not just about you and me. It is like bushfire: you only have control when you haven't lit it. Do you know what Umuachala will do at dawn when they find I'm gone? My people will be smoked out like rodents . . . and impaled in the public square for all to see!

Ifediba: By the blood of kings that flows in my veins, what a blunder! It's an oversight, a dreadful one and it must be fixed immediately.

Ajachi: My prince, if you love me as I love you, just go. Let me be just another lass, one of the hundreds you will conquer on your princely march to the throne of your fathers.

Ifediba *[listlessly]*: Apiti! Where is Apiti? My treasure, you mentioned bushfire. I want it to start burning here and now!

Ajachi: My prince . . . .

Ifediba *[shouting]*: Apiti! Apiti!

[Enter Apiti, vaulting in with acrobatic aplomb]

Apiti: A name in the king's mouth in the deep of night is worth more than a keg of wine. I am that name, Your Highness.

Ifediba: Apiti, this is an emergency and I trust you will handle it well. Send two detachments to Umuachala. Fetch Ajachi's father and entire household this very night. We meet at Umudimkpa by nightfall tomorrow.

Ajachi: Your word is law, Your Highness.

[Exit Apiti. Fade.]

ACT 2, SCENE 1

Throne room at the Umudimkpa palace, midnight.
The three queens in white knee-length cloth tied above the
breasts, stand before the vacant throne, bowl in hand.

Oyidi'a: It is midnight; another week is born. Fellow wives of the Great One, we come before the gods. May we perform the weekly rites of cleansing.

Mmiliaku: White chalk is in my hand, Oyidi'a.

Akwamma: My hand has white chalk. Let's proceed.

Oyidi'a: True we carry bowls of white chalk in hand, but our hearts are not one. Mmiliaku, Waters of Affluence; Akwamma, Egg of Beauty, are we showing by comportment and utterance that we are royal mothers who understand the mood of the season? Behold the throne of our great husband. Must it suffer another week of anxiety? The gods are watching us three and people are beginning to talk. The sacred duty which time and custom entrusted to us as wives of the king must be done in purity of spirit. Our hearts must be united in purpose and prayer.

Akwamma: My heart will never unite in hypocrisy. Oyidi'a, Image of Her Husband, hear me. When the pit of witchcraft is yawning wide, wisdom must beware the kits of deceit. A smiling face and a tongue of flattery will not entice me to embrace a witch.

Oyidi'a: These are bad words, Akwamma. I will not let you speak like that in this place!

Mmiliaku: Let words be said, Oyidi'a. The gods who hear will judge. And whosoever is a witch here, let her be food for dogs.

Akwamma: Ise-e! I say to that. May the gods remove the front teeth of our secret enemies so by their smiles we shall know them.

Oyidi'a: Let me tell you what I know. The gods only fight for those who rise with them to the high ground of goodwill to everyone. This moment is sacred; white chalk is in our hands. We should fill the dawn with cleansers, not curses.

Akwamma: Cleansers have their sure moments. But I spare no curses against the bereaving cry of the midnight owl.

Oyidi'a: I insist on grace in speech and conduct as befits our status. We are queens, not fish wives.

Akwamma: The gods know the pains in my heart. If I seem or sound inelegant, it is the staggering and stammering of tormented motherhood.

Oyidi'a: Are you the only mother here? Mmiliaku, your senior has six to your four.

Mmiliaku: But all mine are female which counts as nothing for the throne. That is why I must endure a life of insult and derision.

Oyidi'a: What about me? Should I take a battle to the gods? Only they can say why they tied up my womb, denying me the sweetest joy of womanhood. I threw years of prayer and sacrifice at every shrine known to mankind. It was all to no avail. Has that turned me into a witch, Akwamma?

Akwamma: What I said was never directed at you. The heavens know that as well as everybody.

Oyidi'a: Silly remarks cannot reverse my open stream of benevolence. I gathered you both as mine, nursed every child born in this palace as my very own. Today, all your children call me mother. No one can take that away from me.

Akwamma: All I've said is that Ogbuagu Ifediba is my son and he will sit on the throne of his father. The witch saying no in her heart shall die like a rat.

Mmiliaku: Oyidi'a, let us do the bidding of the gods. My ears have suffered enough rubbish for one night.

Oyidi'a: I am truly disgusted.

Mmiliaku: It is worse if you know what I know. It is becoming a heavy burden because of frequent provocations but I choose to keep my mouth shut. For the peace of the kingdom and the good name of our great husband, I will maintain the calabash of silence.

Akwamma: Calabash! A stray dog never lacks a neat excuse for the shit in its mouth. Let every calabash be broken. Let everything be spilt in the full market place and let the smell hit us in the face. What is the silence for? I ask. Only one who bathes with her waistcloth on knows exactly what she is hiding.

Mmiliaku: Oyidi'a, you are hearing. Pollution will not stream from my mouth. But I will not yield endless space to a smelly shrew for a dance of spite under my nose.

Akwamma: We shall know who is a smelly shrew. In a matter of days, we shall know who is what in this palace.

Oyidi'a: I will fine both of you for defilement.

Mmiliaku: The rope of justice should bind only the bringer of offence; otherwise it is cheap and loose politics.

Akwamma: All the mindless talk will cease in a few days.

Oyidia'a: Not in a few days, but this very moment, let it stop. We are here, standing before the gods. Let there be quiet and let's perform our duty.

Mmiliaku: White chalk is in my hand.

Akwamma: My hand has white chalk.

Oyidi'a: We make our presentations.

[She lifts up her bowl; the others do the same]

Mmiliaku: White chalk is clean and cleansing.

Akwamma: White chalk is pure and purifying.

Oyidi'a: O you gods whose eyes are everywhere, receive our tokens of peace and purity.

Mmiliaku: Peace and purity.

Akwamma: Peace and purity.

Oyidi'a: This new beginning, this dawn of new hopes
May this sprinkling of white chalk
Like virgin breath of the new-born
Refresh our entreaties.

[They move around in single file, sprinkling chalk powder]

Mmiliaku: We renew our entreaties.

Akwamma: Be renewed, our entreaties.

Oyidi'a: Peace and purity we seek.

Mmiliaku: Peace and purity we shall find.

Akwamma: Peace and purity be our apparel.

Oyidi'a: Life and light we crave.

Mmiliaku: Life and light we shall embrace.

Akwamma: Life and light dwell with us.

Oyidia: Love and laughter fill our land.

Mmiliaku: Love and laughter build us homes.

Akwamma: Love and laughter clothe us pure.

Oyidi'a: Our men shall be men.

Mmiliaku: Our women shall keep home.

Akwamma: Our children shall know the truth.

Oyidi'a: Peace and purity.

Mmiliaku: Peace and purity.

Akwamma: Peace and purity.

[More sprinkling of chalk powder. Lights dim. Exeunt. Fade]

ACT 2, SCENE 2

Throne Room at Umudimkpa palace, long after midnight.
Oyidi'a is meditating, seated on a mat beside the footstool of
the throne, her thoughts floating in a voice-over as her dream
is re-enacted in one corner.

Oyidi'a *[voice-over]:* Last night's dream was so vivid ... Igwe was sitting over there on the throne, his back to all. It was raining so hard with flashes of lightening and loud peals of thunder. I could hear everything Akaeze was saying. But Igwe's words were muffled or mostly lost in the wind. Akaeze was labouring to get around the throne for a face-to-face with Igwe, but an unseen force kept pushing him back.

Igwe: It is Ubulu. Ubulu.

Akaeze: I know Ubulu was your first love. There you encountered that goddess ... Of course, Nwakaego was a goddess. Remember it was those people's first uprising and your maiden campaign on your father's behalf. We were so young then—thorough like sharp knives and only keen to prove that we were ready for Isibuke. We ripped Ubulu apart in just four days.

Igwe: But Nwakaego ripped me apart in just one moment

Akaeze: Ah, Nwakaego is unforgettable. A maiden with the mint of morning and mystery of moonlight. Remember, we were told that she was a princess of the itinerant Aros. But later, when you married and there was no child from Oyidi'a, the oracles said you had a boyhood dalliance with a river goddess and there was a son whom you would never see.

Igwe: Where is my son? Where is my son?

Akaeze: I feel your pain, Igwe, the Great Sky himself. Did we not turn kingdoms upside down, looking for Nwakaego? We dared rock and forest, probed lairs and dens, searched hills and valleys, for the first woman you gave your heart.

Oyidi'a: But where really did Nwakaego go?

Akaeze: Where does a river goddess go? Her affair with Igwe was a whirlwind. Just five days, then she was gone, leaving no trace to this day.

Igwe: Find my son, Akaeze. Find my son.

                           [Fade. Oyidi'a emits a long-drawn sigh]

Oyidi'a: Ah!

                           [The scene fades . . . . . . Enter Mmiliaku]

Mmiliaku: Oyidi'a, pardon my intrusion. I'd been waiting for ages by your hut. I need to talk to you.

Oyidi'a: Join me on the mat. I was reliving the early years of my marriage. Magic years, magic years. I used to sit here at his feet.

                           [Mmiliaku sits beside Oyidi'a]

Mmiliaku: A truly great man.

Oyidi'a: Greatness can never look as great, or Royalty as royal.

Mmiliaku: He deserves better from the gods. Oyidi'a, I feel the urge to sound a warning about Akwamma. Somebody should stop that woman. Otherwise, the whole world will hear things that will make the cesspool look like fresh water.

51

Oyidi'a: Mmiliaku, my dear, should we not avoid these petty squabbles? Madness is not a joint enterprise. My honest advice is—ignore all provocation and childishness.

Mmiliaku: Akwamma habitually pours filth from her mouth. How long am I supposed to keep quiet and stomach her insult?

Oyidi'a: After these many years, you ought to know each other better. Next time she calls you a witch, remind her that we three are in the boat and she is still the junior mate.

Mmiliaku: Her frequent cry of witchcraft is blunt with over-use and no longer bothers anyone. But she has now gone too far, Oyidi'a! Akwamma opened her mouth to make dirty insinuations against me . . .

Oyidi'a: Wear a thick skin, Mmiliaku. Whatever she says to you or about you, brush it off as nothing.

Mmiliaku: No Oyidi'a, not this one. Akwamma said I slept with condemned slaves to have my children!

Oyidi'a *[horrified]:* May the gods spare us all! My ears will not hear such outrage.

Mmiliaku: Oyidi'a, my heart is burning like coal inside of me. I will go public with all her dirty secrets! She will tell what nightly errands that sneaky slave, Otondo runs inside her hut. And she must name the fathers of her own children, if she can tell.

[Oyidi'a rises abruptly]

Oyidi'a: I refuse to hear this kind of talk. I'm ashamed of both of you. Have you too lost your senses, Mmiliaku?

Mmiliaku: You won't sound like this if you know what I know.

Oyidi'a: I don't want to know defilement. And, let me advise you, gauge your words before you speak any further. Words are winged creatures which once uncaged, fly without control, never to be recalled.

[Enter Akwamma]

Akwamma: The words of my mouth have no wish to be recalled. They are arrows of purpose. My son is born to rule.

[Akwamma faces the throne]

Ogbuagu Ifediba! Scion of the Great Lion! Living Friend of High Thunder! I hear your footsteps of destiny. When the forest is abuzz with the chirping of insects, it is because the lion has not spoken. I hear the rush of wind but that is nothing. Only the entry of the lion halts the gallivanting of antelopes. The proof of courage is when the mighty one has roared. Ogbuagu, blazing son of the mystical forests, the throne of your fathers summons you. Arise, son of my womb, prized cub of the great lioness—I tell you what a mother tells her precious child—it is time. Arise and uphold the name of your great father. Enter and rip the masks of jealousy so they mock no more. Tear apart the twisted tongues of talebearers, that the mouths of murmurers be filled with dung. Ogbuagu, Legend of the Caves, Terror of the Hills, Great Stalker who makes the blades tremble, the palace of your father is dressed and waiting, a bride swooning for her groom. Living Friend of High . . . .

Oyidi'a: Akwamma, hold your peace. A lion does not need a litany of names for introduction or the big titles of his ancestors to take his rightful place.

Akwamma: I agree, Oyidi'a. But in a battle with a witch, an invocation is thunder in the mouth of a lioness.

Mmiliaku: A beast that lives on innuendos is dead in guts. It stinks!

Akwamma: The only thing that stinks worse than the fart of baboons is—

Oyidi'a: Hold your peace, both of you. I have had enough of your childish altercations. Since you forget who you are or what you are supposed to be, I will talk to you like infants . . . and I do not want a word from either of you.

Mmiliaku: Oyidi'a . . .

Oyidi'a: I said, not a word. You make me sick, both of you. Was it not a moment ago that all three of us purified the palace? I stayed back here to meditate awhile—this only time that the palace blinks in its eternal watch of the king's wives. A wise woman would use such a moment of gold to bargain with the gods, purchase peace divine for self and family. But here are two royals spewing more muck than piglets in a fetid pond. I feel ashamed, the sounds alone. What dung you smear each other with, I really don't much care. But I swear by my last breath, this earth will not contain you and me if the reek touches my dear husband or any child he called his own.

Akwamma: Oyidi'a. Oyidi'a . . . . .

            [Oyidi'a storms out, rolled mat under her arm]

Oyidi'a: This may be the sleep-walker's last chance

Akwamma: And who is sleep-walking?

Mmiliaku: The one who does not know that once inside a bottomless pit, Lioness is vain title for Dead Cat.

Akwamma: Better worry for the fool who does not realize that when a lioness has a fully-grown male child by her side, she is a goddess.

Mmiliaku: Only a miserable animal fancies herself to be something when the fear of her shameful past is pushing her over the brink.

Akwamma: In a few days, only a few days, we shall know who is what in this palace!

[Fade]

ACT 2, SCENE 3

Throne room at Umudimkpa, morning next day.
Enter five high chiefs. Dikeogu and Ebekuo are chatting,
strolling slowly to their seats. The others go straight, each
slapping his stool with his cow-hide fan before sitting. Only
Akaeze and Ajofia are absent.

Dikeogu: All night long, I could not sleep a wink.

Ebekuo   You took anxiety to bed.

Dikeogu: When serpents run loose in the rafters, who can sleep?

Ebekuo: Ah, I grab my share these days, sitting or standing. And
             I recommend the same to you because this trouble is no
             longer looking like a one-night visitor.

Dikeogu: I detest the feeling of helplessness—sitting all day like
             senile old women, strange events dropping on our laps
             like rotten fruits. It is one bad report after another.

             [They slap their stools with their fans and sit down]

Ebekuo: When I heard that we have come under attack at Isibuke
             of all places, I thought it was a sick joke. I still can't believe
             that Umuachala could do such a foolish thing.

Dikeogu: We still don't know their motive; so don't call them foolish.

Ebekuo: I forget they are your mother's people.

Dikeogu: Affection for mother does not dilute duty to fatherland. I am proud of our response—swift and severe the way it has to be. Umudimkpa is never late to battle.

Orimili: But we cannot afford a full-scale war with Umuachala. They are our cousins from the beginning of time. They never fight us and we never fight them.

Ebekuo: Why then did they invade when they know that Isibuke is sacred to Umudimkpa? Nobody bears arms there except Ogbuagu and his chosen troops.

Orimili: What Umuachala did has no precedent in history and it is difficult to find an excuse or explanation. The timing of their invasion makes their motive even more suspicious considering the strong ties between the two kingdoms. Our army has moved in quick response, ready to strike a telling blow. If a serpent fails to behave as serpent, women would convert him to a string for their waistcloth.

Mmanko: That is very true.

Dikeogu: Isibuke is boiling like a mad pot, with all the maneuverings going on there. But we have it sealed on all sides. No entry, no exit.

Ebekuo: So, how will Ogbuagu come out of that place?

Eto'odike: G-g-gooood q-queee-queeeestion!

Orimili: Clearly a dilemma, but the protection of his life is top priority.

[Enter Akaeze. All rise.]

All: Akaeze! Right Hand of Majesty!

Akaeze:	Akaeze acknowledges his fellow high chiefs. The honour is to the fatherland.
All:	Umudimkpa, the land of warriors!

[All sit after Akaeze is seated]

Akaeze:	Ajofia is not here?
Orimili:	He is expected—after his morning round of the shrines.
Akaeze:	The High Priestess of Isibuke is on her way here to brief us. She requested for safe passage last night and I gave approval on behalf of the throne.
Dikeogu:	That is most unusual. The Isibuke priestess is never to be seen outside her forest.
Akaeze:	Has Isibuke ever seen such a violation of her sacred grounds? These are desperate times, so we must be inventive. The high priestess will come out—and not more than four of her slave women with her. But their faces must be covered.
Ebekuo:	Seems fair enough.
Dikeogu:	We are just letting the whole world turn upside down.
Mmanko:	Dikeogu has spoken my mind.
Akaeze:	Well, somebody should tell us what is better: to let the world turn itself upside down or to let it turn us inside out.
Dikeogu:	I just know that the land is crying out for appeasement. We all know why.

[Enter Echezo and a palace guard. Echezo prostrates]

Echezo: Akaeze, Worthy Hand of Majesty, I covet the dust at your feet.

Akaeze: Arise. Speak to Umudimkpa.

Echezo *[rising, dusts his hands]*: Isibuke greets the palace. The five women have arrived at the gates under close escort.

Akaeze: Bring them in.

Echezo *[to the palace guard]*: Bring them in.

Palace Guard *[cupping his hands to his mouth, shouts to someone off-stage who in turn relays the message]*: Bring them in!

[Enter Ajofia, rearward first. He halts at the staff rack and removes the silencer palm frond strip clenched between his teeth]

Ajofia *[agitatedly]*: Fellow high chiefs, fellow high chiefs, do we now permit masked persons on the palace grounds? Masks right inside the palace?

Ebekuo: Take it easy, Ajofia. That must be the High Priestess of Isibuke and her maidens.

Ajofia: Ewo! Isibuke enters the palace as well? Alas, seven rogue years! The kernel is gone, the squirrel mocked by an empty shell. Where are the paths our ancestors trod in blood and tears, the beacons of counsel that guided the kingdom from age to age? Ajofia feels the anguish of the gods, the dreadful wrath behind their deep silence. The blood cry of appeasement must ring again in this land. Ajofia swears that Umudimkpa shall be men again.

[Enter three hooded women. Each is clenching in her teeth a silencer strip of palm frond and bearing in hand a clay pot of burning oil lamp. Two of the women quickly disrobe, revealing their male identities—Apiti and Ifediba. The chiefs are horrified]

Ifediba *[exultant]:* Men, it's great to be home! Great to be home at last!

Apiti: Great, Your Majesty. Congratulations!

Ifediba: We've done it, Apiti! You are tremendous!

[They trade knuckles, hug excitedly, the chiefs moping in stupefaction]

Apiti: It just boils down to brains. Your Majesty, just trust me. I have the brains to bring the rains.

Ifediba: We outwitted those sons of dogs! I wish I could see their faces now! We played them out.

Apiti: It's just brains, Your Majesty. Anytime. Anytime! *[Whispering]* But see, it's like the chiefs are—shocked . . . I think it's best you address them immediately.

Ifediba: That's right, that's right! *[Turns to the chiefs]* Great High Chiefs!

Apiti: Great!

Ifediba: This is me, live! I'm home at long last and it sure feels great. Please accept my high regards. I appreciate that this is not the usual format of this great occasion. But change is the father and child of progress. As you elders like to say, when the drumbeat changes, a dancer must change his dance steps. The whole world out there is changing pretty fast. My administration will move very rapidly to make all necessary changes. Customs which add no value to life or those that perpetuate darkness and retard progress must be thrown out with finality. We must work together, you and I, to take this kingdom to the next level. I need to thank you for your good patience and the series of emissaries you dispatched to me. The long wait was necessary and worth it in the end. I succeeded in bringing home with me a person without whom my life would have no purpose or rhythm. A snail cannot move without his shell; a lion cannot forsake his mane. I could not leave that amazing forest without the one person whose love takes me to the very sky above, a person whose sheer presence makes me thank the gods for making me a man.

[Pointing to the third hooded figure]

That is my treasure, the next queen of Umudimkpa. Her name is Ajachi. Step forward, honey. Don't be shy.

[Ajachi removes hood and cloak. She is slightly nervous, but stunningly beautiful. She curtsies dutifully]

Apiti: Say hi to the chiefs.

Ajachi *[with a mini wave]:* Hi.

Ifediba: Just look at this jewel . . . this marvelous work of creation, this sublime package, this celebration of quintessential womanhood. We had to break every protocol to snatch her from the baying dogs of tradition. That is the direction of my administration. I need you as fathers to rise with me against the forces of darkness and hate, against the worms of evil that eat a section of the human race alive, and against a past that prefers to bury this kind of goodness in the dungeons of primitive habitude.

Apiti *[applauding lustily]:* Great! That's great!

Ifediba: The change we have begun is irreversible. In my kingdom, nobody shall be called slave. I make this proclamation even before my coronation to drive home the point that my administration will push emancipation far above my father's great legacy.

Apiti *[applauding]:* Well spoken, Your Majesty.

Ifediba: Ajachi's parents are liberated too. Someone bring them in
            so I can round off the introduction.

                            [A cue and a whisper from Apiti]

Sorry, I forgot to introduce my good friend, here. He is son
to one of you (though I don't know what the quarrel is) but
since he joined me in the forest, I've found him a tremendous
asset. He is a thinker, a master planner, a force you prefer
on your side, a nightmare to any opposition, an ever-ready
fixer. We call him by a nickname that best describes his
tricks, since he has dropped his birth names. Apiti, we call
him, the Slippery Mud that Foils The Unwary.

Apiti *[claps and bows]:* Hi, everybody.

                    [No word from any chief. Enter two hooded persons]

Ifediba: And here they come—Ajachi's parents, soon to be royal and
            celebrated.

*[The couple remove hood and cloak, falling on their faces in full, untidy
                        prostration before the speechless chiefs]*

Apiti: The masses must be liberated from such archaic display of
            sickening subservience.

Ifediba: Yes indeed, we must review these fawning manifestations
            of servitude in the new dispensation. What is sanctity of life
            without the dignity of man? Help them to get up.

                        [Apiti assists the fumbling pair to their feet]

Apiti: Your Majesty, the chiefs are not talking. That smells mischief.

Ifediba *[to the chiefs]:* The deep silence of elders—that ancient tyranny
            of fence-sitters—shall have no place in this revolution. Speed
            of execution is a given for all our programmes. But there

must be constructive dialogue—vibrant debates that show passion and commitment. Akaeze, as Prime Minister, much is expected of your leadership of this body. We must drive the change process together. Do you have any comments?

[Akaeze contemplates, considers his colleagues awhile, then clears his throat]

Akaeze: Orimili will respond for us. But before that, I have a question that bothers me. Where is Okafor?

[The chiefs exchange glances, nodding in endorsement]

Ifediba: Oh, that one? His fate is a timely signal, so let all be warned. Every tall grass of tradition refusing to bend to the wind of change is doomed to the roots. Apiti is my witness how I virtually begged Okafor not to go back to the camp. He knew like us all that Umuachala had encircled the place.

Apiti: He refused to listen, said he must recover some missing traditional object, that he couldn't face Umudimkpa without it. Imagine such a brainless frolic right on the battlefield.

Ifediba: They captured him alive, I hear. I'll be glad if they don't hurt him though, because when he isn't boring like a fog and rigid as a corpse, he is not really a bad fellow.

Apiti: Your Majesty, my main worry is that Umuachala may place a hefty ransom on his head.

Ifediba: I will not negotiate with dogs that I will soon chase out of farm, field and forest. There will be neither ransom nor recognition for anyone who goes backward for a relic.

Apiti: Your Majesty, that point deserves to be drilled into every skull. What is an old snuff box that it cannot be replaced with a brand new one? Why endanger life or render the whole kingdom a hostage for some useless relic?

Ifediba: I am putting you in charge of Strategy and Reorientation
           with immediate effect. It is a massive trust, to change the
           mentality of our people.

Apiti: I have the brains to bring the rains, Your Majesty. My first task
           is to make it clear to all that this is a revolution. Everyone and
           everything can be replaced—fiam! like this—except, of course
           the throne of Umudimkpa and its worthy embodiment.

Ifediba *[hugs Ajachi]*: And my precious love, here.

Apiti *[applauding]*: Yes, of course!

                    [Orimili rises, confers briefly with Akaeze]

Orimili: Ogbuagu, Inimitable Terror of the Vast Wilderness, I salute
           your name and the power of your fame. There are three
           kinds of silence and mother cow knows the difference.
           The silence of the plains when the he-lion has roared, the
           silence of death—final and endless, and the silence of bulls
           as they chew to swallow and chew yet again. When a blind
           man listening to a story says 'I see' it is because his mind
           has caught a picture larger than the common canvass of
           words. Ogbuagu, Umudimkpa swallows and cannot be
           swallowed .... all of us know that. But today is a rarity. The
           silence you hear this moment is because weighty words have
           beaten our ears and eaten our mouths. Be assured, however,
           that as you retire to your royal quarters for a deserved rest,
           everyone here will regain jaw and joints. We shall launch
           into those vibrant debates of passion, to position ourselves
           for the revolution. On behalf of Akaeze, the Prime Minister, I
           assure you that the council of chiefs supports revolution. Or
           is anyone opposed to revolutions?

                [General sounds and body language denying opposition]

Orimili: Umudimkpa salutes Ogbuagu. The high chiefs salute you.
           Welcome to the lion's den.

Ifediba: Very well then, your discussion should focus on the situation at Isibuke. My immediate priority is the instant cleansing of that place and the swift liberation of Ajachi's other folks who are still trapped there. Every member of her family shall attend my coronation. That is my promise to her.

[Fade]

ACT 2, SCENE 4

Throne room at Umudimkpa palace, right after.
Ajofia is standing near the staff rack. All other chiefs are seated.

Ebekuo: No, no! This is just a bad dream and happening to me alone.

Orimili: We are in a proper mess. It cannot be wished away.

Ebekuo: Is this a curse or just an age thing?

Dikeogu: Indiscipline has no age grade. Igwe, the Sky-king was a mere boy when he mounted that throne.

Orimili: Youth are different nowadays—difficult to guide. They put their noses in the air like wild dogs and follow their own persuasions. This age has no regard for custom or counsel.

Dikeogu: How can you tell, Orimili? Your son, Obiora is such a joy to parenthood. Look at my own case. You can see what I had to live with and finally disown.

Akaeze: We are in deep trouble. Anyone can now see why Anyandimmuo went dumb before our very eyes. The greatest eavesdropper of spirit talk suddenly clamped up and has not uttered a word till this very moment.

Ajofia: What was he ever going to tell us? Any of us who prefers to plug his ears with broom sticks cannot stop the angry gods from crying out for appeasement. My staff of office is lifted up. This land must be saved. Seventy slave heads!

[He bangs his staff on the floor. Mmanko is swift to join, followed by Dikeogu and Eto'odike]

Mmanko: Seventy slave heads!

Dikeogu: Seventy slave heads!

Eto'odike: Seventy slave heads!

Ebekuo: Are we not rushing a reversal of progress?

Dikeogu: No, we want to reverse the rush of misfortunes.

Orimili: Where is our sense of loyalty? We made a vow to Igwe.

Dikeogu: My loyalty is to the land, my duty to the living.

Orimili: What use is leadership if it shifts like the weather and drifts with the tides? Seven years we pushed this cause—pushed it with the fervency of battle gear till every spilling of slave blood was stopped in the land. Why do we suddenly rouse like bloodhounds at full moon, to bay for seventy heads? We must not infect our people with contradictions.

Dikeogu: This is not about us or the people. It is about the gods above.

Orimili: No one has seen the gods, remember?

Dikeogu: You and I have argued this a dozen times. The gods are seen in all events of life, the pains and pleasures that fall on our doorsteps. When the heavens rain only torments and afflictions, only the naive remains in the open field.

Ebekuo: I warrant that this may sound like Mmanko, but in all truth, Dikeogu is speaking my mind!

Mmanko: Oho!

Ebekuo: The more I reflect on the matter, the more I agree with Dikeogu.

Mmanko: Then, why wait? Join us, Ebekuo. Come and speak with your staff.

Dikeogu: Let us return to the old way, the road our fathers traveled.

[Ebekuo rises, hesitates]

Ebekuo: This is for me, a crossroads. I am being torn apart. My heart remembers our beloved monarch; his dearest life-work is crying out to us like an orphan child, begging for adoption.

Orimili *[solicitously]*: He entrusted that crying child to us. We swore an oath.

Dikeogu: I warned us against that oath!

Orimili: Still, you gave your word of honour.

Dikeogu: If the times dishonour my word, I rethink without apologies.

Ebekuo: And who can fault that in the present situation? My head reflects on the rampage of wild bulls, a craze that takes everything for granted and casts sand in the teeth of elders.

Dikeogu: No respect whatsoever!

Ebekuo: A brashness that brooks no counsel and makes no enquiries

Dikeogu: Trampling on their betters; no reverence for anything!

Ebekuo: Imagine the arrogance threatening to replace everybody.

Ajofia: I am waiting for anyone to dare me.

Dikeogu: Waiting I am.

Mmanko: I too.

Eto'odike: I t-t-too!

Ebekuo: I too.

Orimili: Unfettered youth is vexation to age, and even wrath to
               the gods. But patience is the eternal path of wisdom.
               A reckless fart is very provoking but no reason to plug
               every hole in a domain.

Ebekuo: But it is good enough reason to shift from the spot of
               pollution. I can see very clearly that the only way out of this
               mess is a return to the ordered path of our ancestors—where
               flesh and spirit respect rights and limits, the landmarks are
               fixed and every bird in the air knows his perch.

Dikeogu: We have drifted too far, to a point where further patience
               is madness. We must take action or throne and kingdom
               may fall to slaves.

               [Ebekuo lifts his staff]

Ebekuo: I vote to appease the gods, praying it isn't too late . . . .
               Seventy slave heads!

[He stamps the floor and Mmanko excitedly trades staffs with him]

Dikeogu: Akaeze, your five brothers are standing in the sun.

               [Akaeze fetches his snuff box and slowly takes a helping]

Akaeze: The sky may remove from its place, but as long as a breath
               remains in this aged body, my word to a friend living or

dead shall stand. I will never cast my staff to butcher slaves again—not in my watch, not ever.

Dikeogu: Then, our problem is not what Orimili called unfettered youth. The problem is elders who refuse to use the fetters.

Orimili: How does killing the slaves fetter the youths? I stand with Akaeze.

Ajofia: Ajofia permits himself a little laugh and that is very unfortunate as the gods can fend for themselves. Let no man blame the sky if tomorrow bleeds. The man whose head is used to break a coconut does not join the feast. The place of honour for the loudest cockerel is the steaming pot of soup.

Akaeze: May those threats and curses afflict only our enemies.

Orimili: Ise-e!

Ajofia: When the gods feel cheated of due rations, who can stop them from picking on bystanders? Ajofia will not mourn anyone who would not be warned.

[Fade]

A(T 2, S(ENE 5

Throne room at Umudimkpa palace, that afternoon.
Akaeze is seated—head-bowed, Orimili standing a step away
from him.

Orimili: That Ubulu boy has run away again. It is the third time. The
guards request for permission to chop off his right foot.

Akaeze: Who needs the right foot of a twelve-year old? All I covet
is his potent charm which put our watch to sleep.

[Orimili sits down]

Orimili: Things have never been this bad, Akaeze, but Igwe's
words are still alive: The only thing worse than
walking around a problem is sitting down to admire it.

Akaeze: Very true, Orimili, but Igwe also said that a problem faced
together is a ready feast. Since you are here, Orimili, we
can feast together. Tell me how to get Umudimkpa out of
this nasty pit.

Orimili: What we must do is hasten the coronation. Just push it
through. It's not going to be easy with Ajofia threatening
another boycott, this time all the other high chiefs with him.

Akaeze: It is no longer a threat. They sent me word just a moment
ago that the palace has been replaced as our meeting
place. It is in furtherance of Ogbuagu's revolution. They
would sit in Ajofia's place until I agree to pacify the gods
with seventy slave heads.

71

Orimili: No! no! no! That is right back to the pit of savagery!

Akaeze: Aren't you starting to admire the problem?

[Orimili rises to his feet]

Orimili: No, Akaeze. Not even this should defeat us. I will stand by my vow to the king, even till death.

Akaeze: I appreciate your sense of honour, Orimili, but it is only two of us now. How do we run against five? And how do we stand with reckless youth?

Orimili: It is a challenge but we must follow the footprints of the ancestors or be lost in the storm. I am going to engage all the elders one by one—knock on every door and speak to every heart.

Akaeze: The gods gave you the great power of words even from the womb. The elders will listen like charmed snakes. But what about the youths? Their world is a riot of deafening noises. They are indifferent to the melody of reason.

Orimili: They will listen to one of their own. My son Obiora is very persuasive and his mates flock to him.

Akaeze: That boy is a jewel. I wish every young man is like him. But who knows, he may be the next Akaeze in Umudimkpa.

[Enter Apiti]

Apiti: Akaeze, is this the debate you all promised the whole world? Where are the other chiefs? You sit here plotting next appointments into Ogbuagu's cabinet? That is absurd. Let me warn on his behalf, if this is a pastime around here, it must stop with immediate effect. This revolution will not tolerate such speculative trade in stools and titles nor condone any underhand manoeuvering or conspiratorial gimmickry which breeds needless tension and acrimony in the community.

[Orimili in rage, jumps to his feet]

Orimili: Young man, get out of here!

[Akaeze is visibly seething; leans back, eyes closed]

Orimili: Get out, I say!

Apiti: Hey, no problem. Just chill. I'm leaving, all right?

[Heads towards the exit. Enter Ifediba]

Ifediba: What's going on?

Apiti: Just what I warned you about. I caught them red-handed, but if they say I must go, I go.

Ifediba: No. You stay. Akaeze, what's the matter again?

Akaeze: I will not dignify that rascal's impudence with any comment. He has no business here. I've got to talk to you.

Ifediba: In that case, both of them shall leave.

Akaeze: This is Orimili, a high chief of Umudimkpa.

Ifediba: And this is Apiti, a key member of my inner council. Disrespect for him is disrespect of me.

Orimili: Never mind, Akaeze. I will leave. Don't forget it is a revolution. Anyone can be replaced.

Apiti *[whispering to Ifediba]*: It's show-down time. You are crown prince. Take charge. Don't let an old cow push you around.

73

[Exeunt Orimili and Apiti. Ifediba draws a chair across and sits at an angle to Akaeze]

Ifediba: Look Akaeze, I say this with due respect—I expect more maturity than I am getting from you and the chiefs . . . .

[He pauses. Uncomfortable silence]

Ifediba: You are not saying anything . . . . I don't want to be rude . . . . but, when you elders adopt this attitude of not speaking, it makes conversation a fruitless monologue . . . that's very frustrating . . . and it's unfair.

Akaeze: What do you want me to say, Ogbuagu?

Ifediba: Look, Akaeze, the kingdom is under severe stress. Isibuke is boiling. Umuachala is daring us as no one has ever done. We need to teach them a bitter lesson and I need your cooperation. Is that too much to ask for?

Akaeze: You don't need to ask for my cooperation. It is there for you. I expect us to discuss in earnest, arrangements for the funeral and coronation.

Ifediba: The coronation must wait. I want you people to always listen when I'm talking. My priority is Isibuke, didn't I make that clear? I want full military action.

Akaeze: You only have personal command of the army upon your coronation. Until then, power lies with the council of chiefs.

Ifediba: Then rally them as Prime Minister.

Akaeze: It is not as easy as you think.

Ifediba: You are denying me the support I need.

Akaeze: No, you are making support impossible. Your approach has alienated the high chiefs. I am here, just hanging in.

Ifediba: You make it sound like I am the problem, but it is you elders that resist change and reject progress. How long do you think I'll tolerate that?

Akaeze: The tongue in every mouth knows the secret of harmony with sharp neighbours. I advise you to learn that secret. You cannot run alone.

Ifediba: Am I not the one asking for cooperation here?

Akaeze: The soft tongue in our mouths does not ask for cooperation. Yet our sharp biting teeth work with it in perfect peace and harmony.

Ifediba: This is getting diversionary. The usual tricks! I am talking of serious matters; you shift to tongue and teeth! Look, Umuachala is killing fellow human beings. At least five persons are butchered every day. Have we no courage to stop the carnage and unite both kingdoms?

Akaeze *[with a mirthless laughter]:* Ogbuagu, a boy can never father a son ahead of his own parents. In case you haven't noticed, your coronation is going to be a big battle. Let's fight that battle and win it before we look for another war.

[Angry voices within, in heated exchange. Enter Orimili and Apiti in obvious agitation]

Orimili: Akaeze! Desecration! My eyes have seen desecration! Akaeze, the virgin of peace is raped!

[Akaeze springs to his feet]

Akaeze: What is it? What is it?

Orimili *[with reference to Apiti]:* Let his own mouth narrate what he has done.

Apiti: What have I done that I will not do again and again? If they bring more stupid eggs, I will break them all.

Orimili *[resignedly]:* He has broken the egg of peace.

Akaeze: The gods are numbered!

Orimili: Umuachala sent peace but this worthless animal blocked the messengers at the gate and broke the egg.

Apiti: Please don't call me names. What is all the fuss about? It's a common egg, come on!

Akaeze: You son of the wind! What do you think you know about anything? That egg was peace if we returned it whole with a lump of white chalk.

Ifediba: All right, all right, the egg is broken. How do we go forward?

Apiti: It is open war. The broken shell is clear signal that we mean business here. Umudimkpa says no to vultures and will not accept an egg of cowardice.

Akaeze: And who are you to speak for Umudimkpa?

Ifediba: It's all right, Akaeze. He has my authority.

Apiti: The king's authority is absolute. Let's move this kingdom forward.

Orimili: I can't believe this is happening.

Apiti: It's a revolution. Let's be progressive.

Akaeze: Ifediba, this reek and ripening is beyond hook and pole. Enough is enough. Akaeze moves to put a final stop to all pretensions. There is ownership in every land. You are not yet king of Umudimkpa.

Apiti: This is open treason, Your Majesty.

Ifediba: From a man supposed to be my father's closest friend and confidant.

Akaeze: I have not seen in you any bit of the great man whose friendship shaped every step of my adult life. All I see is a presumptuous lurch, one giddy step after another, a drunken insect determined to bring death on itself and everyone. Ifediba, enough is enough. You are not king yet; and when you become, Akaeze will mind the ropes.

Ifediba: Akaeze, I had respected you as my father's friend, but this open challenge is unfortunate and you will regret it.

Orimili: Threatening a man your father's age is not wisdom. When a boy rudely carries up his father in a fight, his eyes are blinded by dangling objects.

Ifediba: I am just fed up with all these ancients. Let's go, Apiti. My response shall be ruthless.

Akaeze: Our response to your response will be simple. But it will show that king and kingdom belong to the people.

[Fade]

ACT 3, SCENE 1

Throne room at Umudimkpa palace, late noon two days after. Seated on low stools in a corner are Ifediba, Apiti and Chime.

Ifediba: The kingdom is strung up like a kill about to be quartered. Daggers and drills on every side. Where will this end?

Chime: Obiora's peace campaign has calmed nerves on both sides. It's amazing.

Apiti: Should we accept castration in the name of peace? You must take charge, Your Majesty.

Ifediba: What can I do now? This Akaeze man has shut down the palace on me. Even the domestic staff now ignore my orders.

Apiti: There'll be pay-back on pay-day. I am marking everybody.

Chime: Let's give peace a chance. Obiora has consulted every blade of grass in the land and his open dialogue idea is uniting youths and elders.

Ifediba: The fellow has done great, truly surprised me. I dismissed him at first as just another loose-feather dreamer.

Apiti: But what exactly are we celebrating in him? There is peace of war and there is war of peace; and there is peace that is needful and peace that is evil. We must know what we want lest we deceive ourselves and swim in evil peace—a vile lake that swallows the brave and smiles at the indolent.

Chime: I'm not quite sure I understand your flow. Are you suggesting that war is better than peace?

Apiti: I am saying—and very clearly too—that we must move with the speed of youth. Why drag and dither like tired old women? Speed is the power of lightening. Speed is the only edge of youth in the generational battle of wits. Except we speed off, the aged, the weak and the sick will tie us in their loin-cloth. Is that how I want to spend my life? What peace can there be in a jungle when the lion is starving? Our comrades are still trapped out there at Isibuke. My heart is breaking for Ajachi's siblings. If peace delays their release, I vote war.

Chime: But Obiora is negotiating their release and there is progress.

Apiti: Negotiations can take for ever. The name of this game is speed. Sex with a mad woman is best grabbed as a quick one.

Chime: That sounds like a lot of experience.

Apiti: Chill. Let's just use our brains—strike now when the iron is red hot.

Ifediba: Where are the troops? Don't you get it? I don't have a command yet.

Apiti: So, we arm the slaves!

Chime: Apiti!

Ifediba: Is that a joke? Wait . . . . . That's an exciting option.

Apiti: That is the move of the moment, Your Majesty. It is the substance of dreams. Empower slaves to fight for their own freedom, an army unstoppable is born. Just say yes, Your Majesty. Give teeth to the revolution.

Ifediba *[contemplates, turns to Chime]:* What do you think?

Chime: I sense trouble, Ogbuagu. Expediency may look harmless like an egg but it often hatches serpents. Apiti says give teeth. But if house rats grow dog teeth overnight, who is safe?

Apiti: Leave old goats to worry about that. Let's focus on speed and procure arms before nightfall.

Ifediba: I think I like the boldness. It is quite exciting. But I need to consult a little more. Call Otondo here, and Ajachi's father too.

[Enter Akwamma]

Chime: Ah! Here comes the mother royal.

Apiti: Would Your Majesty need some privacy?

Ifediba: No, you stay, both of you.

Akwamma: They must leave for now.

Ifediba: I say they stay.

Akwamma: They have mothers, don't they? I want to talk to my son.

Ifediba: Mother, how many times must I repeat that I do not want your intrusion.

Akwamma: Intrusion! Who brought you into this world? *[Sits on a stool]* You will hear what I have to say though you are king or soon to be. I carried you in this womb for nine full months and you had nothing to say about it.

Ifediba: You should have aborted me then, and saved yourself the obvious embarrassment which my personal choices are causing you.

Akwamma *[tearfully]*: Hear the way he talks to me. I'm just like nothing to him. Since he came home, he has shut me out . . . I can't get a single moment with him . . . . You, his friends, is this how you treat your own mothers? Why don't you ever advise him?

Apiti *[whispering]:* Your Majesty, you don't want a scene here. Release us and manage her.

Ifediba: One thing I will not tolerate is anybody holding me to ransom. I will not bow to sentiments or succumb to lemon tears.

Apiti *[whispering]*: Still talk to her. Mothers must be petted, like infants. What matters is not what they feel but how they feel.

Ifediba: All right, both of you may leave. But stand by to meet me with those two men.

                              [Exeunt Apiti and Chime]

Akwamma: Ifediba, my beloved son, the enemies of my peace of mind will never locate you.

Ifediba: Mother, you have your moment. Don't waste it.

Akwamma: Ifediba, my son, I am not here to quarrel with you. I have come to beg you. See, I am on my knees. *[Kneels down]* It is life that I am talking about. Your life, my life.

Apiti: Why are you trying to embarrass me? Please get up.

Akwamma: My knees remain on the floor. If that is the only way I could get your ear, let me even crawl. *[crawls]*

Apiti: Look, mother . . . I'll just walk out of here if you don't stop this.

[Akwamma gets up]

Akwamma: My son, will you be heartbreak to your only mother? Ifediba, you are my jewel, the pride of my life, my eagle. Do not allow enemies a habitual perch on my head. Do not make room for useless people to mouth my name in derisive wine songs. This shame is killing me. Ifediba, I am dying in torment.

Ifediba: You are old enough to die, mother if that is what you choose. All I owe you is a decent funeral and you will surely get one. Please cut out the drama and say what you need to say.

Akwamma: Ifediba, the evil spell of witchcraft can never destroy your mother's love for you. Enemies are desperate to steal your heart, breed harsh words in your mouth and blind you against me, but all that will fall to the ground because you have a mother who will fight the gods for your sake . . . My son, have you heard the latest street song?

Ifediba: What street song?

Akwamma: Of course, the affronted is usually the last to hear. They are singing it everywhere . . . . Even infants have joined the outrage. You can hear it, can't you?

[Singing within]:

'Onye kpo nkita ba n'uno
Chupu ya, chupu ya
Oga akpotalu anyi eze nchi
Eze nchi ewe mee anyi alu'

Akwamma interpreting each line:

83

'Who brought home a mongrel dog?
Chase it out, chase it out
Lest he next brings king of rodents
King of rodents could wipe us out'

Ifediba: Where is your name in that?

Akwamma: Can't you see? It's about that girl.

Ifediba: Mother, let me just warn you again. That girl is not your business. There will be no hiding place for anybody on this earth who speaks one bad word again about Ajachi. I have gone to the boundary of the spirits over that girl. She is my choice and what I have dared to bring her here should tell the whole world what she means to me.

Akwamma: What can she mean to you, Ifediba? Which brave hunter discovers the great assembly of birds and targets the little *nza*? Every girl in this wide world is on parade for you, my son. You can have any princess, any daughter of a quality family. Even the married ones will quickly forsake their husbands and go with you. But see, you forget who you are.

Ifediba: I forget nothing. Who on earth can forget when Akwamma wants something? You want me to be king, and king I shall be—but never one who breathes from your lungs and sees with your eyes. This king will not be slave to anybody's expectations. I must rule my own life, the better to rule the kingdom.

Akwamma: So, it is all for spite? You went through a world of plumage and brought me this nameless thing—not even a person but the lowest of the low, a foreign slave girl!

Ifediba: You are my mother; so I spare you a choice. Either you shut your mouth on this matter or I shut my ears against you for ever. This is either the last time we talk about this or the last time you see my face.

[About to storm out]

Akwamma: This is not empty-handed. Witchcraft has caught my son. They have turned the treasure of my life into an arrow to my heart.

[Ifediba stops in his tracks and returns]

Ifediba: And get this, mother. There is no witchcraft in my love for Ajachi.

Akwamma: Maybe it is the gods themselves . . . Or the ancestors. It's like they are getting their last laugh . . . . after all these years. My son . . . perhaps I should have told you all these years. I should tell you something very important.

Ifediba: I don't want to hear anything about anything anymore. Let me simply dwell on Ajachi. She is my valley of joy, a woman who makes me feel so complete I salute the gods. You do not know the meaning of treasure till you feel the thrill of her touch and the warmth of her embrace. I have traveled lands and rivers, seen shades and colours, felt flames, flowers, flavours; but Ajachi is the pilgrimage experience. My voyage of self-discovery is a gaze into her eyes.

Akwamma: Ifediba . . .

Ifediba: Let no one expect me to give her up. The melody in my heart is one with hers. That is all that counts to me.

Akwamma *[hoarsely]*: Ifediba . . . . Ifediba . . . .

Ifediba *[conciliatorily]:* Mother, if you have ever experienced the exquisite pain of true love, simply wish us well. Do not mind the empty chorus of mudslingers so blind they mess

85

with gold dust. I who mined this gift of nature shall refine it to class before your very eyes. Tomorrow I tell you, is an ornament and a better song.

Akwamma: Tomorrow? There is no tomorrow. I see a curse. A curse!

[Gets hysterical]

It is the ancestors! I hear them laughing. They are laughing in my ears, in my head? Is it your head? Ha! Ha! Ha!

Ifediba: Mother, are you all right? Mother!

[Akwamma falls into a fit, stripping frantically]

Akwamma: Ifediba! Ifediba! They are laughing, laughing! Can't you hear them? Whose ancestors? Do they know you? Ha! ha! Do you know them?

Ifediba: Somebody get over here quickly! Mother!

[Akwamma struggles on the floor, screaming as Ifediba battles to hold her down. Apiti and Chime rush in, followed by two palace guards. In the background the song 'Who Brought Home the Mongrel Dog' floats. Lights dim . . . . Fade.]

ACT 3, SCENE 2

Throne room at Umudimkpa palace, that evening.
[Enter palace guard, whistling 'Who Brought Home The
Mongrel Dog'. He inspects every corner and returns to the door
to usher in Ajachi and her parents, Ibenibe and Nwamgbeke]

Palace Guard: You may come in. Over there is fine, yes there. Stand right
there and wait. He will soon be through with his mother.

Ibenibe: Thank you, master.

[Palace guard takes sentry position]

Ajachi: Father, relax. Nobody will hurt you here.

Ibenibe: How can you tell? Why is he calling me alone? I insist you
and your mother keep close to me always. I don't trust
that man.

Nwamgbeke: We cannot trust anybody. But the man is very nice. I like
him but I am feeling terrified.

Ajachi: There is no cause for fear. I've told you everything. I am
pregnant for the Crown Prince of this great kingdom and
he has promised to marry me.

Ibenibe: You even believe that kind of talk. Is the fellow mad or it
is you that have the wind in your head?

Ajachi: Father, why are we here? Is it not he who took all that risk
to deliver us?

87

Ibenibe: It is not deliverance, my daughter. This is the attack. Whose wife did I look at or whose yam seed did I break that they should pick me and my family for destruction? See my armpits; they are bare. I stand when my fellows stand and sleep where allotted to me.

Ajachi: Father, you should really be excited. This is a great privilege. Don't you want to be free? These people who are free, do they have two heads?

Nwamgbeke: The man is very nice. He will do it for us.

Ibenibe: What pigeon heads are women! You believe too much. The wind passes, you believe him; a leaf drops, you believe it.

Ajachi: Father, this man is special. His love for me is real and he will do anything for me.

Ibenibe: Shut your mouth! See the trouble your day-dreaming has brought upon us. Have you never heard that Umuachala does not spare? Princess Ugochi will hound you to the end of the earth and gouge out your eyes. As for me, they will tear me limb by limb. Who will believe that I knew nothing? I was abducted in the middle of the night, taken into the forest with all my family, brought in masquerade clothing to a place I don't know. What freedom is that?

Ajachi: Any freedom is better than bondage.

Ibenibe: It is the empty head of your mother in you that uttered such foolishness. Didn't the gods favour you in the land of our birth? You were the envy of every slave girl as personal maid to the princess. Ugochi herself treated you well, often gave you gifts—even for me.

Nwamgbeke: That is true and she gave me too. But this man is very nice.

Ibenibe: How can you forget who you are? By what name of juju did you think you could sneak behind the princess and snatch her stool from under her very buttocks?

Nwamgbeke: A baby is coming. It will make the man even nicer.

Ibenibe;   That is your foolish imagination and that is why you did not tell me about this thing. You knitted it in secret like an amulet for the private parts, and Ajachi wore it in silence from me. This mess could have been avoided. I would have married her off to any of her many suitors.

Ajachi: Then, my baby, a royal seed, would have a slave father?

Ibenibe: Shut your mouth. What is the root of peace in community? Is it not discretion? If every woman insists on the actual father for every child, many slaves would be princes and our world upside down.

Nwamgbeke: Be careful how you talk in this place.

Ibenibe: I am talking of wisdom here. A wise woman chooses whom she announces as her child's father.

Ajachi: I have chosen the right man, father.

Ibenibe: Ajachi, your choice has put me on the run like a bandit. Your brothers and sisters are hiding like hunted animals at Isibuke. Umuachala does not spare. I fear the worst for my poor children.

Ajachi: Father, my prince has made special arrangements for the safety of my family. He won't even commence his coronation until all my people arrive here.

Ibenibe: Is the fellow under a curse?

Nwamgbeke: The man is very nice.

Ibenibe: How will Umuachala believe that I had no hand in this thing?

Ajachi: Father, stop worrying yourself about Umuachala. Umudimkpa is our new country and you will be a great man in this place. We are welcome here, father.

Ibenibe: If yours are shut, my own eyes and ears are wide open. I see their mean masks and I hear the wicked song they sing and whistle everywhere. If that is the welcome, we are dead and buried.

[Voices within—Anizoba and Otondo trading words]

Anizoba: I am not a slave!

Otondo: You are even lower than a slave, you idiot!

Anizoba: You are hurting me. Why are you hurting me?

Otondo: I haven't even started. You will suffer for all your stubbornness. And, let me warn you; don't make noise inside this palace!

[Enter Otondo, dragging Anizoba by two ropes, one handcuffing Anizoba's wrists, the other his ankles. The first is tied to Otondo's left wrist, the second, his right ankle, so his movement in any direction pulls the boy along. Ibenibe and his family watch in silent horror]

Anizoba: You don't like hearing the truth. But I know I am not a slave.

Otondo: So, what are those decorations on your wrists and ankles, just like mine?

Anizoba: Ropes do not make a slave. I am a prince of the Ubulu kingdom. Ahh! You are hurting me again!

Otondo: You must go where I go, do you understand? You and I are tied together because we are slaves . . . and because I am now your minder full-time.

[abruptly tugs on the ropes]

Anizoba *[in pains]:* Ahhhh!

Otondo: You brought this on yourself, see? We used to move about freely and you and I could go our separate ways. Then, your madness came, and this is the result!

Anizoba: Ahhhhh! Stop! Stop!

[Ibenibe leads his family to the door. Ajachi speaks to the sentry]

Ajachi *[to the sentry]:* My father will wait outside

Ibenibe: All of us.

Ajachi: Yes, all three of us will wait outside until the prince is ready for us.

[Exeunt Ibenibe and family]

Otondo: If you don't want pain, you must go as I go. You brought this upon yourself by your stupid attempts to escape. Many times I warned you but you would not listen to the voice of experience.

Anizoba: Ahhh! You wicked man! Stop! Ahhh!

Otondo: Child, this is just playtime. Sunset is coming; they swing the axe kpom! your right foot goes.

Anizoba: The gods will never let them do that to me.

Otondo: Leave the gods alone. They never bother themselves with the cries of slaves.

Anizoba: I don't believe you. The gods are doing their best but there is too much wickedness in people.

Otondo: You are just a child. What do you know about anything?

Anizoba: I know what is good and what is bad. I know it is not good to suffer one affliction and inflict ten on others.

Otondo: What words are filling your mouth? What are you talking about?

Anizoba: Every pain in this world is caused by people. See what you are doing now—pulling the ropes to hurt me!

Otondo: Am I the one that made you a slave?

Anizoba: I can never understand your kind of grown-up person. You seem so contented, even happy to be a slave.

[Otondo sits dejectedly on the floor]

Otondo: Nobody on this earth wants to be a slave.

[Anizoba walks over, squats beside him]

Anizoba: So, why do you accept it? Why are you doing nothing to change your position?

Otondo: You cannot fight the gods. Only they know why they made some people free to live and others to serve or die. My father handed me one secret code of happiness: make the best of what you cannot change. If I must be a dead man, I'd be so dead that the grave would cry louder than the mourners to have my body.

Anizoba *[thoughtfully]:* It's a strange kind of wisdom and it makes a lot of sense. But what do you gain from a half-life?

Otondo: You are still a small boy, but if you can keep a cool head, you will catch on very quickly. The farm work here is good and you'll soon find that bending down is much fun. You can sow seeds in the most reserved gardens and eat of the best fruits. It is very exciting when you learn to speak with your eyes and keep your mouth shut.

Anizoba: I think that farm work is the same everywhere. You can't sow cassava and reap yam.

Otondo: You are a bright kid all right but you have not learnt to look stupid. How do you expect to live long?

Anizoba: I can never accept to act like a slave if that is what you mean. I am a prince of the Ubulu kingdom. I'll rather die than be like you.

                    [Otondo gets up angrily and pulls the rope]

Otondo: You stupid next amputee! You servant of slaves! You harmattan haze of a dreamer! You still think you are better than anybody?

Anizoba: Ahhh! Sorry, sorry, sorry boss.

Otondo: What did you say?

Anizoba: Ahh! I said sorry.

Otondo: What did you call me?

Anizoba: Boss. You are the boss here.

Otondo: Good. You are learning fast, see?

Anizoba: See, you are not the problem. We both are victims. Why can't we work together and make the pains lighter for each other? Let's be friends, boss.

Otondo: I like it when you call me boss. It's very nice. But I warn you, the only way we can be friends is when you stop making trouble. Stop all that foolishness—running away, planning to escape, boasting you are prince. Forget where you are coming from. Umudimkpa has you here. You are a slave like the rest of us.

Anizoba: Boss, it is not about me alone. All of us can be called princes if we refuse to be called slaves. Why do we allow fellow human beings to put us in pits and cages? Let's stand for our dignity, one for all and all for one.

Otondo: Anizoba! A child must learn that growing up does not mean climbing up to the sky to pluck the stars. Kid dreamers like you destroy the peace of ages. You pick a flickering flame and start racing against the winds. It is defiance of the gods. A wind may snuff out your light point blank or fan a flame to consume the whole world. Is that what you want, kid? Or shall we just look stupid and let tomorrow come?

Anizoba *[after reflecting awhile]*: Let tomorrow come, boss. *[Aside]* But what kind of tomorrow?

[Lights dim. Enter Ifediba and Chime. Otondo goes flat in prostration but Anizoba remains standing]

Otondo: Scion of Thunder, my head burrows in the sand for safety. Lofty Branch of the Great Iroko That Covers The Heavens, my eyes are shut than get blinded by the splendour of your presence!

Ifediba: I did not ask you to come shackled. And who is this one with the arrogant stare?

Anizoba: I am a prince of the —

Otondo: He is a new slave boy, Your Highness. His right foot tries
             the rope for my life.

Ifediba: Separate yourself from him and return here quickly. I
             want to talk to you alone.

Otondo: Prowling Lion of the Rain Forest, there is no hesitation
             when you command, but I am only a trapped animal and
             the hunters are watching my tail.

Chime: Don't be impudent. Get a guard out there to untie you. Simple!

                        [The sentry at the door strolls over]

Palace guard: It is not simple at all. Only Akaeze gives orders here for
             now. This is his order and he alone can reverse it.

                [Ifediba is flustered, struggles to regain control, finds a seat]

Ifediba: All of you may leave. Everybody! Not you Chime. This is
             open embarrassment. Call Apiti for me. Call him quickly.

                        [Exeunt all but Ifediba. Lights dim. Fade]

ACT 3, SCENE 3

Throne room at Umudimkpa palace, late evening.
Lights are dim. Ifediba paces listlessly.

Ifediba *[aside]:* Akaeze wants to reduce me to nothing! He wants to
show me that I am nothing.

[Ekwe begins to sound in deep throaty beats]

Ifediba *[aside]:* They are playing the palace *ekwe* even without a word
to me. What's the message? *[listens]*

Ekwe *[with voice-over]:*

Which shrine do you trust with a piece of meat in a night of
starvation?
How does a rhino wear his horn to please a wedding assembly?
What but the nervy rush of peril is a thrill on the hill?
The throbbing heart of panic is drumbeat to the brave

When the burning bush thickens with smoke
Who would swear by crouching silhouettes, who would swear?
Who can restrain the blind arrow of haste in a mad rush for
trophy?
The rearing spear is strike-head, deadly as cobra

Why do the hills exult like hands of praise, fingers skywards?
Which jubilant trees hum silently like sated labour in restful
evenings?

96

Ifediba *[aside]:* I hear you wood major, heartbeat of the fathers. You were there, you saw things for yourself and whenever it matters you call our feet to war!

Ekwe *[with voice-over]:*
> What amulet lies buried in the silence of deep valleys
> That hawk and kite like docile doves sentence themselves in guilt?
> A term of drift and repeat circles, shadows of pain engaged
> Ablution is no use to a procession of swamp pigs
> Hear the soft paw of sunset; quickly stow the eggs of dawn
> Retreat is not cowardice, but the winning step is forward
> Summits do not faze monkeys; limits cannot strip the wind
> When caution gets dizzy, giddy is long lost
> Away with the calabash; upwine is no friend . . . . .

Ifediba *[aside]:* There can't be two heads on one neck. Akaeze must go.

[Enter Ajachi]

Ajachi: My prince.

Ifediba: My treasure . . . You are the only piece of sanity in my life right now. Come, my balm of love.

[They embrace and drift to a corner bench]

Ajachi: My father waited all evening for your call.

Ifediba: It's been a very bad evening. I'll still see him though.

Ajachi: He is very worried. Please be nice to him—for my sake.

Ifediba: There's no reason to worry. I'm going to make him a high chief.

Ajachi: My father—a high chief?

Ifediba: Yes, my love. But first there is a fight that can't wait. The old prime minister must go.

Ajachi: I thought he was your friend. You always said he was your father's right-hand man.

Ifediba: Childhood friend and playmate, lifelong ally and confidant, but now he blocks my way, mocks me from behind a mask and stabs me in the back. Apiti warned me about this. It's a bad mistake to trust any old man.

Ajachi: Whatever you do, please be very careful. I am having terrible nightmares. I have not been sleeping well at all.

Ifediba: My treasure, it is good for me that the old fox has come out openly to hunt. There is nothing to fear. In a cobra hunt, the hunter is the hunted.

[Ajachi is pensive; she rises and moves slightly away]

Ajachi: It's been one battle after another. When will they stop?

Ifediba *[standing beside Ajachi]*: Battles don't count, my love. Victories do, and I intend to claim all. Young is smart, swift and special, right? Old is exhausted, exposed, expired, ex-everything.

Ajachi: You always try to comfort me—that's one of your sweetest qualities—but please never underrate the danger. We have too many enemies. Have you heard their song?

Ifediba: I promise you they will chew their own tongues. Just go ahead, plan big for our wedding. It is going to be the high point of my coronation.

Ajachi: I love you, my prince.

Ifediba: I won't trade you for the whole world.

[They embrace. Ajachi removes a beaded band from her hair]

Ajachi: Wear this, my prince, for my sake and for your baby. It will bring you good luck in all your battles. Always remember our lamp of love. It is burning in my heart like an everlasting flame.

[She helps him wear it on her left upper arm. Enter Oyidi'a]

Oyidi'a: Ogbuagu Ifediba.

Ifediba: Ah, high mother. I first must apologise. I haven't been to see you. My home-coming has been like a fire outbreak here.

Oyidi'a: Ogbuagu, that fire is burning very badly. We must find quick wisdom to put it out. I have side-stepped custom to come uninvited because things are not going well at all.

Ifediba: Relax, high mother. Battles do not deter the brave from the summons of destiny.

Oyidi'a: True, but braves who appreciate their destiny do not fight needless battles. Is this the girl everyone is talking about? She is beautiful.

Ifediba: High mother, you are incomparable and without bias. No other person in this kingdom has spoken one nice word about my Ajachi.

Oyidi'a   Ogbuagu, wisdom is the noiseless water you need to douse the raging fire. Time is not your friend. Go now and make peace with Akaeze. You need his fatherly guidance.

Ifediba: You don't know that man, high mother, beyond his pretences. He is a stalker, a shameless bully and a spineless opportunist.

Oyidi'a: You need that man on your side, whatever you think of him. Seek audience with him tonight and make peace. The head of prostration does not stick to the floor.

99

Ifediba: Let me be forthright with you, high mother. There is no place in my cabinet for that dirty old fox.

Oyidi'a: You have no right to call an elder bad names. It is bad manners and you are not blameless yourself. Your behaviour is puzzling all and annoying not a few. A willful bird that drops seven mounds of ordure from the sky will not find a welcome perch on the ground.

Ifediba: Akaeze is an ingrate, a man who has forgotten so quickly all that my illustrious father did for him. He is not worthy of my handshake. I can do without him and I will.

Oyidi'a: Ogbuagu Ifediba, the *ekwe* sounded a short while ago. The message is ominous, or did you not disrobe the words? All high chiefs will come before the king at sunrise tomorrow to register their common grief. Ifediba, this never happened in all my forty years with your father. It is open disagreement with the palace.

Ifediba: High mother, what more proof do you need that Akaeze is a chameleon? My father who installed him on that stool is not even laid to rest yet, but he is showing his true colours in a stinking hurry. I will show him what lion and lightening have in common.

Oyidi'a: Your mother is a more urgent matter. Can I have a moment with you alone? It is very urgent.

Ifediba *[drawing Ajachi firmly to his side]*: High mother, my Ajachi is already a full part of me and whatever I need to know she deserves to hear.

Oyidi'a: Ogbuagu, your mother's condition demands your personal attention. She falls into fits and her strange words can endanger you and everything.

Ifediba:	But you know Akwamma even better than I do. She can do anything to get what she wants, and what she cannot get she wrecks without qualms. At every important moment of my life, she lets me down but you've always found a way to pick me up.
Oyidi'a:	I fear this time, it is much more than that. Get to her bedside and stop the words.
Ifediba:	No words can pull the hair off my skin or change the blood of kings that runs in my veins.
Ajachi:	My prince, words have ruined more lives than all the fires of this world. Please do as high mother says.
Ifediba:	You know I will. High Mother and I have come a long, long way matching wits. Yes, because not even she is free from that incurable disease of all parents!
Ajachi:	All parents have a disease?
Ifediba:	A terrible disease, my love. Parents never notice when their child becomes a grown-up that can choose his own fights!
Oyidi'a:	Ogbuagu, are you seeing your mother now or shall I get them to bring her here?
Ifediba:	I will see her, high mother, but if she messes with me at this critical stage, I will strangulate her myself. I swear.
Ajachi:	Please calm down, my prince.
Oyidi'a:	You must do nothing rash. Whatever is happening, she is still a king's wife.

Ifediba:	Am I not a king's son? Why is everyone trying so hard to make me feel small? What is the conspiracy between Akaeze and my own mother?
Oyidi'a:	That throne is a sacred trust, Ogbuagu Ifediba, and everything will stand or fall in the shadow of the ancestors. Go, attend to your mother.

[Ifediba storms out, Ajachi hurrying to keep in step with him. Oyidi'a hesitates, then makes her exit. Lights dim. Enter Apiti and Chime furtively]

Chime:	Did we have to hide?
Apiti:	High mother Oyidi'a? I'd rather take raw-hide scourging than suffer her tongue lash again. Even at this age, she would still pull my ear like when I was a toddler.
Chime:	I never thought your rebel spirit knows a stopper.
Apiti:	High mother, Oyidi'a! Ah ya! ya! ya! Friend, the only person who never minds a boss is a corpse.
Chime:	This is a revelation I will not forget. But, what are we to do now?
Apiti:	Just run and tell Ogbuagu that we've sorted out his mother.
Chime:	You haven't told me what you mixed in that drink.
Apiti:	You ask too many lame questions. This is His Majesty's Secret Service. Tell Ogbuagu that his mother has fallen asleep and it is better not to disturb her.
Chime:	Apiti, is that woman dead?
Apiti:	Am I the spirit that created her? I prefer she stays out two/three days.

Chime: Suppose she dies.

Apiti: Suppose she went on mouthing obscenities? What's wrong
            here? Someone has to fix things like I just did. Please
            inform His Majesty that everything is under control.

                                                    [Exit Chime]

Apiti *[aside]:* Moralizing is weakness, a taboo to a hunter. Like hesitancy,
            a timid walk in unlit tunnels, every breath is laboured, a
            burden of too many probing questions, few definite answers.
            The viper suffers no morals; his only answer is venom which
            he pours on his victims, leaving them all the questions. Is
            he not nature's example to guide youths to battle exploits?
            Apiti, you have done well, whatever they say. This is brains!
            Superior tactics!

                                                [Re-enter Chime]

Chime *[breezily]*: Congratulations, man! Can you believe the news?

Apiti *[eagerly]*: Some old hog is dead?

Chime: This is about us, man. It is straight to the throne, the
            dream team complete! Complete without a fight! The
            Isibuke captives are home!

Apiti: You aren't kidding. How did that happen?

Chime: They just arrived. Ogbuagu is celebrating.

                                            [Enter Okpijo and Ebili]

Okpijo: Someone, just rush me food! Any food at all, bring it or I
            swallow somebody.

Apiti: Okpijo himself! Evil Prawn That Thrives Only In Combat!

                            103

Okpijo: I hear you, Apiti. Bring food.

Apiti: Evil Child That Entered His Mother's Womb Through The Alleyway!

Okpijo: People, bring me food.

Ebili: For me, bring palmie!

Apiti: Ebili, Stormy Waters That Test The Canoes, I greet you.

Ebili: My calabash will greet back when refilled.

Apiti: You will eat and drink all you want. This is a celebration.

Ebili   You never know the pull of home
Till you are stranded and alone
Or lost upon a distant shore
The last boat long, long gone

Okpijo *[yawning heavily]*: Men, home without food is a grave. Bring me food.

Ebili: When the only bridge is broken and the last boat is gone
And the lonesome trooper shambles on the shore all undone
A swim with crocodiles or the drowning plunge the reckon
The setting sun is signal that home is a dream of heaven

Okpijo: Or a bowl of food! Who is bringing me something to eat? I'm starving.

Chime: If you can't wait a decent while, I'll take you to the kitchen.

Okpijo: Which one is called decent while? I'm just coming out of death. Take me to the kitchen or wherever food is ready.

[Exeunt Chime and Okpijo]

Apiti: It must have been the mother of battles. How did you break out?

Ebili   They let us go. There was no fight.

Apiti: How?

Ebili: You know it's just us, the youth royal hunters. How many are we—forty-eight? Umuachala are good fighters—they threw the numbers at us, cut us off and pinned us down for days. Okpijo was raving for a charge—that was obvious suicide, so we restrained ourselves. Things got tough. Food stock was running out . . . Then yesterday, they just came with white cloth and tender palm frond, and they let us go—even escorted us to meet Umudimkpa troops.

Apiti: Then we have a major problem.

Ebili: How?

Apiti: Peace does not fall from the sky. It is purchased at a price, often a terrible price.

Ebili: Well, I don't know what Obiora did to achieve our release. I only heard it took days and nights of close meetings with the elders here and there.

Apiti: We have been sold. Like cheap goods, we don't even know the price of sale, just let Obiora mess up our destiny.

Ebili: Why do you talk like this? Our mate has achieved without bloodletting the peace that no blind rage or bloody battles can ever deliver.

Apiti: This is the peace of poison. It should make us panic, not celebrate. Obiora is a day-dreamer. Who knows if he has sold half the kingdom?

Ebili: Whatever he has done, the people support it. All the way to the palace gate, jubilant crowds followed us singing in solidarity.

Apiti: People are stupid.

Ebili: Thinking so is worse

Apiti: Did you listen really well to their song—the one about mongrel dog? *[He shoots furtive glances, then sings it in a whisper]* I'm sure you don't know the hidden mischief. Who are they calling mongrel dog? *[more furtive glances and a whisper]* It's Ajachi.

Ebili: That's unfortunate. But the tide changes the moment she pleases the people. We must help her to win the people over.

Apiti: The insult must be stopped. We must identify the instigators and deal with them.

Ebili: Force can never win the battle for the hearts of men. Let the country flower with songs. Delight or derision, let every petal find a garden and let hearts in freedom light the open sky.

Apiti: So let Obiora become a god. Then you and I should jostle with the crowds for an inch of space to worship at his feet. Can't you see the dirty fingers of the old toads in all this? They are playing Obiora against us his age mates, to offend Ogbuagu. Can you hear that stupid song again? How do you want His Majesty to feel about it?

[The singing gets much louder . . . . Re-enter Ifediba, followed by Okpijo and Chime. Okpijo is eating hungrily from a steaming bowl in his hand. Chime has two bowls and hands one to Ebili]

Ifediba *[taking his seat]*:   Obiora is like a bad tooth. Of him and Akaeze, I wonder which pain is worse.

106

Apiti: Your Majesty. I warned you about Obiora and his vaulting ambition. His father has been scheming to foist him on you as the next Akaeze.

Ifediba: Even the lowest stool he will not smell as long as I reign on the throne of my father. Let the rabble invent more idiot chants. Obiora will be lucky if I don't banish him for life.

Okpijo: Your Highness, a bad tooth should not be banished, but extracted.

Ebili: Shouldn't we move elsewhere for these discussions? Walls have ears, as they say.

Apiti: Let walls and ears worry that they cannot stop Ogbuagu. The king must reign from this palace no matter what Akaeze feels about it.

Ebili: What has Akaeze to do with my preference for the open fields? This place gives me the creeps of unseen shadows as if the open liberty is a covered bait. My father used to say that everything in the home of a warrior is a security man and even the ostensible absence of guards may be the ultimate trap!

Ifediba: I will not live in fear of my shadow, but I never impose my brand of boldness nor expect anyone to dare beyond his own courage. All I ask for is loyalty without which friendship is fake and life itself an empty walk. Akaeze should come and uproot me if he wants me out of the palace. But anyone who has no fight in him let him leave now.

Apiti *[stepping quickly to Ifediba's side]:* Not even death can separate us, Your Majesty.

Okpijo: Where you stop, I die, Great Hunter.

Chime: We have a strong team here, Ogbuagu. Everyone is loyal and committed.

Ifediba: Speak for yourself. People are being used against me. They are singing idiot songs out there against me. My own mother says things no one wants to relay and I can't get it from her. This is war. I can no longer assume anybody's loyalty.

Apiti: It's Akaeze, the old fox and his boy, Obiora. Just imagine the insult in that song. It is treason.

[loud singing of 'Mongrel Dog']

Ifediba: Immediately after my coronation, I will replace that man, Akaeze.

Apiti: Your Majesty, we should sack the entire council of chiefs. They are deadwood. Let's inject new blood into the cabinet—young people who can run with the vision of the revolution.

Chime: We must be careful. It's not like soup licking to remove a single high chief.

Okpijo: Anybody can be thrown away. I can throw anybody out of the palace, single-handedly.

Chime: Real power never throws words about. Ebili, sing for us that great song about the iroko.

Ebili *[holding out his empty calabash]*: Fill my calabash and logic will flow.

[Chime takes the calabash]

Chime: I love the lyrics of that song:
           'Every high chief is an iroko tree, a great iroko tree

Unnumbered birds in the many branches make their nests, make
their nests
How can you fell an iroko and not vex the birds?
How can you fell an iroko and not vex the land?
A stump becomes an idol, a pit will draw lament.'

Chime: The moral of that song is this: once you kick one high chief, a
            whole world of birds, worshippers and mourners go singing
            against you.

Okpijo: Bone! Remove one bad tooth and all the singing will stop.

Ebili: The birds of heaven sing toothless, my friend. We can woo
            them to nestle with us, and the singing will be on our side.
            This is our moment of cross-over. The people should be
            celebrating with us, not chanting against us.

Apiti: Ebili, you are too sober to make any sense this evening.
            Chime should quickly fill that calabash, so you can amplify.
            Tell us how it is our fault that Obiora and his father are
            plotting with Akaeze to undermine Ogbuagu.

Ebili: Apiti, more drink than anyone else is what you need to
            manage the lunatic children of your marriage to mischief.
            But, seriously, let's all have a nice drink and begin to plan
            how to make this coronation ceremony a delight to the
            people.

Ifediba: You are not in the Planning Committee.

Ebili: Oh, there is a planning committee?

Ifediba: Of course, there is a plan group. You are not in it because I
            am no longer sure of your loyalty.

Ebili: Is this a joke, Your Highness?

Ifediba: Should a king joke with matters of state? That exit door awaits anyone whose loyalty leaves a shadow of doubt.

[Okpijo moves instantly to Apiti's side]

Okpijo: His Highness will not repeat himself. You have to leave.

Ebili: No, this has to be a joke. I to leave? How? What? Why? Where . . . . where am I to go?

Ifediba: Follow where you please. The open fields . . . the wonder sky . . . . the toothless birds . . . you know where.

Ebili: No, Ifediba, a lifetime of friendship is sacred; it cannot be wiped off by one sigh of happenstance or misjudgment. You and I roamed the wilds, combed the thickets for honey and romped home with the joy of kid monkeys, the angry bees whizzing past our ducking heads. A nobility of spirit held us together and though we watched out always for each other, we never spared ourselves the brutal truth in any situation. I have never betrayed a friend nor been false at the shrine of fellowship. You and I have come to this point where we need each other most. Why are you shutting me out?

Ifediba: Boyhood is over.

Apiti: Sad, but very true.

Ebili: Ifediba . . .

Ifediba: Make no further speeches.

Okpijo: Move or I move you.

[Ebili moves dejectedly, stopping to retrieve his calabash from Chime. Exit.]

Apiti: That was superb, Your Majesty. A king must project strength and power.

Ifediba: It is just a signal that I expect you all to sit up from now on. I deserve and demand unquestionable loyalty. I hope that is clear. *[Singing of 'Mongrel Dog' is heard loud]* This insult must stop. Somebody has to stop these bastards!

Apiti: Your Majesty, I'm going to fix it my own way.

Ifediba: What is your plan?

Apiti: Your Majesty, it is classified information, for your royal ears only.

[Ifediba waves off Chime and Okpijo]

Ifediba: Excuse us awhile.

Apiti *[whispering conspiratorially]:* Your Majesty, your enemy is using Obiora against you. I don't know who else he might soon deploy. We have to be extremely careful with all these people. And we must change our strategy since war is not happening immediately. Let's act peace and finish the coronation, then we strike.

Ifediba: That song is upsetting my woman and I would not endure one more night of it.

Apiti: Your Majesty, the singing can change this very night. That is as easy as *nsala* soup. All this noise will turn to funeral songs if two or three of the ringleaders don't wake up from sleep.

Ifediba: I will not have anybody killed in sleep. That is cowardly.

Apiti":   They won't be killed, Your Majesty. They just die in sleep. Neat.

Ifediba: How?

Apiti: They enjoy a good drink, then fall asleep.

Ifediba: The drink is poisoned?

Apiti: Not poison, Your Majesty. Just herbs. Nature's work of roots and leaves from the forest. A powerful medicine man made it for me under oath that I would use it only against the king's enemies. I tested it on him and he died instantly. Your Majesty, this is the real power. All your enemies are dead at a nod from you.

Ifediba *[pensively]*:   Is this what you gave my mother?

Apiti: It was necessary to keep your mother quiet. She was saying horrible things that ears must not hear.

Ifediba: Is my mother dead? Am I being told that you killed my mother?

Apiti: Your Majesty, what she drank—what Chime and I actually gave her—is the knock-out dose only. That's a whole thumb-scoop less than the killer dose. I believe she would be up in two or three days, except you decide to finish her off.

Ifediba: Suppose I decide to wake her up this very moment?

Apiti: I won't advise that, Your Majesty; but the anti-dote is still with me, if that is your choice. It has not been tested but I learnt that a single drop in each nostril hits the brain direct. I can't tell what the reaction would be.

Ifediba: . I will not consent to kill my own mother. You will bring her up before midnight and surrender your entire stock of this substance to me. Otherwise, I will never trust you again.

Apiti *[prostrating]:* Your Majesty, as my commander-in-chief, One who kills a man on the sweetest day of his life, you have to be the rightful custodian of this most potent drug? I will gladly hand it all to you but first, let me quickly attend to the Queen Mother.

[Exit Apiti]

Ifediba *[aside]:* A most dangerous fellow. How much of him is needful and how little is enough? How soon must come a parting of ways; what happens when it comes?

[Ifediba sits, stands, paces listlessly, as two off-stage voices assail him, one from each side]

Apiti: Be mindful of our so-called friends.

Ebili: Be mindful what you ask friends to do for you.

Apiti: If you have to kill, kill.

Ebili: Why on earth would you want to kill anybody?

Apiti: Anyone who cannot kill for you is not a true friend.

Ebili: Anyone who kills for you will kill you.

Ifediba *[aloud]:* Enough of killings. Dying is bad enough. Why can't we just have love in this world—spread the goodness to everybody?

Ebili: Love is the sap of life that runs in every being.

Apiti: Love in old people is like a dry well. The only love they know is dry fish.

Ebili: Love is no different from madness; you bleed in the eye just to prove that yours is special and there is none like it.

Ifediba *[aloud]*: But what I feel for Ajachi, no man has ever felt for a woman.

Ebili: I'm sure you heard the chuckles. Love is an ageless game of ages that many have played long before you and me .... these elders you see around us . . . forget their wrinkled smiles and wizened looks. Each one of them is an ex-champion! Our shrunken sires were once stallions of strength; these shriveled grandmas were gazelles of elegance; and their romantic sorties were the envy of the twinkling stars above.

Apiti: Love is the perfect excuse for a man and a woman to take off their clothes in a hidden place.

Ebili: Love is like a garment. Some find it, some fake it, some flaunt it, some fashion it to fit . . . but everything must fade.

Ifediba *[aloud]*: My love for Ajachi can never fade. The drenching rain will only brighten the speckles of a guinea fowl; the rumblings of night can never halt the stirrings of sunrise. Today is a storm but tomorrow belongs to the sunshine of our love. I shall be king and she my queen.

Ebili: Remember this if nothing else: To be king is to die to yourself and to live for your people.

Apiti: To be king is to take charge. Deal with Akaeze or he will deal with you.

Ifediba *[aloud]*: Apiti is right. I don't approve of some of his methods, but he is right most times in matters of strategy. I should give him a free hand .... Akaeze must go! And this idiot song must stop. I must put a stop to it!

[very loud singing of 'Mongrel Dog'. Enter Ajachi]

114

Ajachi *[flustered and tearful]*:   My prince, why are they doing this to us? Even the palace staff are singing it in my face.

[Ifediba steps forward, hugs her]

Ifediba: Leave everything to me, my treasure. Tomorrow I face the high chiefs and present my demands.

Ajachi: I've been thinking, my prince. High mother is right. Please go and make peace with Akaeze.

[Ifediba pulls away]

Ifediba: My treasure, I give you the world, but spare me that old fox.

Ajachi *[clinging to him]*:   My prince, you need that man on your side. Every man needs a father.

Ifediba: My father is gone. No man can ever take his place. He was the noblest of nobles, the elect of all kings. When I remember that his royal blood flows in my veins, I feel like a giant and every problem on my way is like an ant under my feet. Akaeze is a loser. Tomorrow you will hear.

[Ajachi clings to him, pats the band on his fore-arm lovingly, rests her head on his chest. Lights dim. Fade]

ACT 3, SCENE 4

Throne room at Umudimkpa palace, early morning, still twilight. Enter Apiti and Okpijo.

Okpijo: The woman bolted. They say she's taken refuge at the Agbala shrine. How am I to blame about that?

Apiti: She was entrusted to you. Why did you let her escape?

Okpijo: Did I let her? She broke loose.

Apiti: Chill. Are you telling me that a woman worsted you, Okpijo?

Okpijo: You left the bad job to me alone.

Apiti: Once she sneezed and woke up, my own part of the job was finished. You were supposed to mind her. Are you not Okpijo, Lobster That Wrestles the Waves and Thrives in Combat . . . . Strongest man in the whole kingdom?

Okpijo: Bone! That was not a woman. Akwamma was the power of seven bulls.

Apiti: I've never heard a human being scream like that.

Okpijo: What of the kicking, biting and scratching? See my whole body; my skin in tatters. You talk of screaming.

Apiti: Man, your wounds will heal quickly; but all that rot from her mouth, what is the remedy? She is destroying everything.

Okpijo: Nobody should believe that type of rubbish.

Apiti: The whole world is so hungry for scandals, people feast on wicked rumours. Why won't they believe shit in the mouth of a king's wife?

Okpijo: People must be reasonable. The woman just ran plain mad.

Apiti: Watch your mouth, Okpijo! That's a king's wife.

Okpijo: Is she not better mad than guilty of those wrongs she is confessing so loudly? She swore by the ancestors that she slept with slave men and got them killed after; so all her children for the king are slave-born.

Apiti: Your mouth, Okpijo!

Okpijo: It's no longer a secret. People are talking everywhere and even the song has changed from 'Who Brought' to 'Who is The Mongrel Dog'. You can hear it out there

[Both cock their ears and listen to the chant within:]

> *Onye bu nkita no b'eze*
> *Chupu ya, chupu ya*
> *N'oga akpota lu anyi eze nchi*
> *Eze nchi ewelu mee anyi alu*

> *Who's the mongrel dog in the palace*
> *Chase it out, chase it out*
> *Lest it attracts king of rodents*
> *King of rodents to wipe us out*

Apiti: This is what happens when wisdom buries something and sentiment goes and digs it up. A mess that should be resting in peace is now embarrassing the whole kingdom.

Okpijo: I am not going to stand by and watch them insult our man. One fellow sang that song to my hearing. The slap I gave him has set up a wicked ringing bell in his ear for the rest of his life.

Apiti: How many people are you going to slap? It bothers me that I am the only one doing all the hard thinking in this country. I am putting too much stress on my brains. It's not fair.

Okpijo: But I'm the only one doing all the hard job beating up people. I'm doing it extremely well and I'm improving by the day.

Apiti: So, why haven't you done Obiora? Can't you see that every day he breathes is reducing our man?

Okpijo: I promised to get him before the week runs out, but he is not back from Umuachala. His case is not a problem. It's Akwamma I need your orders. Should I go and finish her off?

Apiti: Hmmm. She's a king's wife and she is taking shelter with Agbala. We have to be careful.

Okpijo: Bone! We cannot allow her to keep saying bad things.

Apiti: Don't be an outsider that mourned louder than the bereaved. This is a family matter. Akwamma has a second son, Ifediba's only brother.

Okpijo: Umunna is a little boy; but he has the temper of a mad ox. He is too prone to violence.

Apiti: I think he should be told where to find his mother.

[Lights dim. Exit Okpijo]

Voices *[singing within]*:   *Onye bu nkita no b'eze*
Chupu ya, chupu ya
N'oga akpota lu anyi eze nchi
Eze nchi ewelu mee anyi alu

Apiti *[aside]*: Except we fix this chant, Ogbuagu will hang someone . . . maybe his very self.

[Enter Chime]

Chime: Apiti, we must speak to Ogbuagu very urgently.

Apiti: Further speech is treason! Chime. You and I must act to save our man. Have you ever seen a chanting mob like this on the palace grounds?

Chime: They are waving palm fronds to support the peace deal. Akaeze is receiving a secret envoy from Umuachala.

Apiti: Obiora killed us.

Chime: It is not Obiora. We need to talk common sense to our man—if it's not too late already. He must forget Ajachi or lose the throne.

Apiti: He might get neither unless we help him to have both. I'm sure you heard of his mother.

Chime: The other reason we need to talk to him.

Apiti: What the situation needs is action, not words. This is war—us against them. Bad things are happening to us and we are just watching, forgetting what superstition does to our people. They'll soon be telling themselves that the gods are against us because we are youth rebels.

Chime: They are already mouthing unspeakable things and naming us one by one.

Apiti: We must do something drastic big and fast; a big evil must happen to the elders too; otherwise, you and I are done for.

119

Chime: I don't understand. Are we to invent evil on people?

Apiti: How come I'm the only one doing all the hard thinking in this country? It's too much stress on my brains. If you boys don't want to do things like men, let's disperse.

Chime: What are you griping at? Am I not doing my bit? Is there anything I've been asked to do that didn't get done? Where did I fail Ogbuagu in anything?

Apiti: Chime, failure is not an option in this matter. The high chiefs will meet this morning in a big way. They should enjoy a special palmwine filled with nature's goodness. *[Fishes out a wrap of the herbs and hands it to Chime].* Be a man, Chime, do something for king and country.

Chime *[stunned]:* Does Ifediba know about this?

Apiti: Of course, he knows everything about the herbs. Be a man and play your own part, right? And . . . . hey? not a word to anyone.

[Lights dim. Fade]

ACT 3, SCENE 5

Throne room at Umudimkpa palace, still morning.
Akaeze and Oyidi'a stand talking at a corner as palace
attendants put finishing touches to a redecoration of the
throne and the palace.

Akaeze: Your husband is a strong man. Even from beyond, he is foiling those who robbed him in life.

Oyidi'a: The protection of his good name is my main concern. Akwamma's case could be an attack of madness which can happen to any human being.

Akaeze: The Akwamma thing will only strengthen decisions already taken. I have sent to the Agbala shrine to confirm what we heard. If it is true that she has indeed sworn the fugitive's oath, then she has elected to become an untouchable—which implies that she knows what she is running from. That cannot be madness, Oyidi'a.

Oyidi'a: Are we then to accept that my great husband is childless? That even the daughters of Mmiliaku are also strangers? I am still in shock, Akaeze.

Akaeze: The early years were not blind, but we were too young to accept what we could not comprehend. Remember the oracles? They were definite that there would be no more child for Igwe than Nwakaego's boy child.

Oyidi'a: The son he would never see.

Akaeze: The son we still haven't seen.

Oyidi'a: So where are we going to find him now? And how can we go about it?

Akaeze: Oyidi'a, you were a great pillar of strength to Igwe in his lifetime. The elders have resolved that you would present the king's kola and palm-wine to the council of high chiefs this morning.

Oyidi'a: As if Igwe is seated on the throne.

Akaeze: Yes, Igwe is alive (may he reign for ever!) His mortal remains will be quietly interred tonight, but there shall be no announcement, until his true son or grandson is found. This was the main decision last night.

Oyidi'a: Last night? Isn't the meeting for this morning?

Akaeze: As true elders, we resolved our differences in the dead of night. Our meeting this morning is only for form's sake. Kingdom is people as Igwe would say.

Oyidi'a: What about these children? They must not come to harm. Whatever is alleged, they were born in this palace and Igwe loved them all.

Akaeze: Children did not ask to be born. We shall keep that in mind.

Oyidi'a: What about Ifediba?

Akaeze: The royal snuff box is missing, Oyidi'a . . . . Is that not what should bother us? The high chiefs are arriving. Please arrange for the kolanuts. And include alligator pepper because it never embarks on a shameful mission.

Oyidia: As Akaeze pleases.

[Exit Oyidi'a]

122

Akaeze *[aside]* : A true wife and a real woman . . . .

[Male voices singing in the lobby off-stage]

Ebunu mmili magbulu n'uwa
K'anyi gaanu fu
K'anyi gaanu fu
K'anyi gaanu nene

Ebunu mmili magbulu n'uwa
K'anyi gaanu fu
K'anyi gaanu fu
K'anyi gaanu nene

> *Ram that has drowned in the rain*
> *Let's go and see*
> *Let's go and see*
> *Let's go and witness*

[Akaeze, steals a dance step, grabs his staff and joins the chorus. Exit Akaeze. The singing gets louder, approaching the stage. Two guards block the way as Apiti tries to enter]

Guard: You cannot enter. The high chiefs are coming in.

Apiti: Are you a stranger here? Don't you know who I am? Son of a high chief and member of Ogbuagu's Supreme Council—I have a double right to enter.

Guard: I have my orders. Nobody goes in without clearance.

Chime: This palm-wine is for the high chiefs. Are we to keep it here or you want to take it in yourself?

Guard: All right, be quick. Be very quick.*[allows Chime in with a big calabash]* Keep it over there. No, not there. In the corner . . . Yes.

[Chime places the calabash in the corner. He looks morose; Apiti is in high spirits]

Apiti *[to the guards]*: Don't mess with me. I am the only person in the
        whole kingdom with a double right to enter the palace. I am
        coming back and I will enter anytime I want.

*[Exeunt Chime and Apiti as the high chiefs garbed in white and bearing
their staffs file in, singing. The procession dances around the throne
room and stops before the rack]*

Akaeze: Kingdom is people.

All: Kingdom is people.

[They all trade greetings with their staffs and hang up]

Orimili: This is a glorious moment, the first time in seven years that
        all seven high chiefs are touching staff in full greetings.

Ajofia: Your son, Obiora made it happen. Is there anyone here who
        is not proud of him? Mark my words, the gods have chosen
        that boy for something special.

Ebekuo: When a boy of that age achieves such a feat of persuasion
        that lion and lamb are drinking from the same bowl, we must
        take note that wisdom is not a preserve of the ancients.

Akaeze: It is the essence of this kingdom that is celebrated above
        everything. One young man is somewhere, rearing to destroy;
        another steps out, determined to redeem. The heavens have
        raised yesterday's boys as today's men to help us stand.

Dikeogu: We teetered so dangerously close to a needless war, ready
        to savage each other's throat . . . The youths that pull elders
        from the brink of suicide shall delight in old age.

All: Ise-e!

Dikeogu: Those ones who are desperate to push elders over before their time will plunge head-first ahead of time.

All: Ise-e!

[All grab their staffs and stamp on the floor]

Dikeogu: Umudimkpa, land of warriors will never lack the rain of wisdom.

All *[stamping on the floor]* Ise-e!

Eto'odike *[intones and all join]:* Eb-bu-bunu mmili magbulu n'uwa . . .

> *Ebunu mmili magbulu n'uwa*
> *K'anyi gaanu fu*
> *K'anyi gaanu fu*
> *K'anyi gaanu nene*
>
> *Ebunu mmili magbulu n'uwa*
> *K'anyi gaanu fu*
> *K'anyi gaanu fu*
> *K'anyi gaanu nene*

Akaeze: Fellow high chiefs, our meeting this morning is to inform Igwe, the Sky-king, of a stubborn ram that is perishing in the rain. The ram has refused all entreaties to accept any form of shelter; now we have a report of a drowning; what are to do with this ram?

All: *Ebunu mmili magbulu n'uwa*
K'anyi gaanu fu
Onye ebuna ya n'obi   *Let none keep him in mind*
Onye ebenalu ya akwa   *let none grieve for him*

Ebunu mmili magbulu n'uwa
K'anyi gaanu fu   *Let's go and witness*
Onye ebuna ya n'obi   *Let none keep him in mind*
Onye ebenalu ya akwa   *let none grieve for him*

125

Akaeze: Kingdom is people.

All: Kingdom is people.

Akaeze: Let's be seated. Orimili will convey our morning greetings to the king's household.

> *[All hang up their staffs and take their seats]*

Orimili *[shouts, facing the living quarters]:* People of the king's house, it is a beautiful dawn. Is the king up from his royal sleep?

Oyidi'a *[within]*: The king sends his royal greetings to his worthy chiefs and subjects.

> *[Enter Oyidi'a, right behind a maid bearing a platter of twelve kola nuts and three alligator pepper fruits. All rise.]*

Akaeze: Oyidi'a, mother of all.

Oyidi'a *[curtsying]*: Akaeze. Fathers of the kingdom, the face of the sky is beautiful in your presence.

All: Oyidi'a, great mother.

> *[The chiefs sit as the maid kneels before Akaeze]*

Oyidi'a: Friends of the king, I stoop in respect and present his kola of goodwill and trust.

Akaeze: Igwe has done well to send kola. Is he up yet?

Oyidi'a: He is a little indisposed and needs a little rest.

Akaeze: You will sit with us and be his eyes and ears.

[A chair, slightly lower than the throne, is brought in and placed beside the throne for Oyidi'a. She sits]

Akaeze: Kingdom is people.

All: Kingdom is people.

[Akaeze picks one kola nut and holds it up as the maid moves round, each chief laying a right hand endorsement on the platter]

Akaeze: Oyidi'a. Fellow high chiefs, kola has entered my hand.

All: Akaeze.

Akaeze: My prayer will be brief as the gods already know the fire in our bellies. May the risen sun smile on the breaking of this kola; may we eat health, power and wisdom to increase in seed and fruit. May the world we leave for our children be better than we met it, and may they not ruin the legacy by conceited indifference or presumptuous haste. We shall be strong always to do what we have to do and to finish what we begin. May the gods honour these petitions.

All: Ise-e!

[Akaeze breaks his kola and two others, dropping the lobes on the platter.]

Akaeze: Oyidi'a, mother of all, you will take a hand-out of kola. *[Oyidi'a accepts the offered lobe from Akaeze]* This is for your peace of mind. You will reign with Igwe, and you will live to finish the work.

All: Ise-e!

[Oyidi'a regains her seat as the platter is passed round, each chief picking a lobe and reserving one whole nut. Exit the maid]

Akaeze: Where is the palm wine?

Oyidi'a: Udoka whom I sent to fetch it is taking some time. Oh, it's there in the corner. Like he just dropped it there and took off.

Dikeogu: That is youth of nowadays. Never finishing an assignment! One will fetch but another must be found to pour.

[Enter Echezo, briskly fetching a gourd. He hauls the calabash before Akaeze and, squatting on his haunches, pours a bit of wine to rinse the gourd,and empties the dirt on the floor, away from all. He shakes the calabash and pours a good measure which he holds out to Akaeze.]

Akaeze *[accepts, then returns the gourd]*: Taste it for soundness.

[Echezo takes a tentative sip, then drains the gourd]

Echezo: This is the goodness, Akaeze. Excellent wine.

[Hands a full measure to Akaeze]

Akaeze *[letting a few drops of libation]:* What we prayed with kola we repeat with wine. May we drink life.

All: Ise-e!

Akaeze: Oyidi'a, mother of all, this is for life.

Oyidi'a *[takes a sip, then drinks deep]:* Thanks, Akaeze. This is sweet enough to kill.

Akaeze: So fill mine to the brim. Let me put life in this tired body.

[All are served and they drink lustily, except the third man, Dikeogu, who declines at first. Apiti appears at the door]

Orimili: This is top quality wine.

Ebekuo: They don't tap like this anymore.

Dikeogu: Since everyone is bubbling in praise, serve me my own share.

            [He drinks and smacks his lips with satisfaction. Enter Apiti]

Apiti: High chiefs, see for yourselves, my father has emptied his cup. He drank it to the last drop, leaving nothing for his very son. Is that custom? He had a good last chance to let bygone be bygone, but see now, he has lost it.

Akaeze *[angrily]*: Who allowed this creature to get here? Guards! Guards!

            [Two guards rush forward to grab Apiti]

Oyidi'a *[on her feet instantly]*: No, Akaeze. Please, please, no fight. No fight at all. He can have the whole calabash. Let him just take it and leave.

Apiti *[snatches the calabash from Echezo]*: Thank you, high mother. We are your sons always. Ogbuagu is with us in the lobby, waiting to be called. We too deserve a drink, don't we?

Dikeogu: Let every ear hear this again from me. This thing is not of me. I repeat, I don't know this creature!

Apiti: Rejection does not bother the vulture. It is the corpse that should bother and we shall see.

Akaeze: Get that drunk out of here!

            [The guards grapple with him but he brushes free]

Apiti: Chill, you pimples. Get on the right side of history now or sorry you will be very soon. Very, very soon!

            [Exit Apiti between the guards]

Akaeze *[still visibly upset]*: Summon those guards.

Echezo *[cupping his mouth with both hands, shouts]*: Guards!

[Re-enter both guards]

Akaeze: Why did you let that fellow in?

1st Guard: He pushed his way in, Akaeze.

2nd Guard: He's been making so much trouble all morning, insulting everybody. He says he is a member of Ogbuagu's Supreme Council.

Akaeze *[chuckling]*: Supreme Council!

2nd Guard: We are trying hard to keep your order never to fight any of them.

1st Guard: But this one is asking for trouble. He even seized the other palm wine.

Orimili: Which other palm wine?

1st Guard: The one Udoka brought. He said you already had one going and it is bad upbringing for high chiefs to be getting drunk so early in the morning.

Akaeze *[sighing with a brief mirthless laugh, shakes his head]*: All right, I've heard. Get back to your duty posts. And be more attentive. Nobody comes in again without my orders.

1st and 2nd Guards: As Akaeze pleases.

[Re-enter Apiti]

1st Guard: You again!

Apiti: Chill! Just looked in to say goodnight to everybody. But it doesn't seem like nightfall yet. What's wrong?

2nd Guard: The fellow is drunk.

1st Guard: Drunk? He's gone mad!

Apiti: Something is not happening. Chill! Something is very wrong.

                              [Exit Apiti. The guards stand at the door]

Akaeze: Kingdom is people.

All: Kingdom is people.

Akaeze: The business of the day is counting time on us. Umudimkpa
          is waiting to hear the *ekwe* as we speak with our staffs.

Ebekuo: There is no dissent about Igwe, and none about Umuachala.
          The only stalemate is our five against two for seventy heads
          to appease the gods.

Orimili: Is there still a stalemate? We resolved as the king lives (long
          may he live) that his gift of life to slaves should stand unless
          the gods reverse it by themselves.

Ajofia: Remember, that concession went with a clear warning.
          Those who deprive the gods of their due sacrifice expose
          themselves as ready sacrifice. Ajofia will not mourn anyone
          that will not be warned.

Orimili: The comments are noted.

Dikeogu: I shudder after what our eyes have seen these past days and
          weeks, that any of us still wants another language from the
          gods.

Ebekuo: Plain language, Orimili said.

Orimili: Are we resuming the debate? This matter is settled.

Ebekuo: We are clarifying our understanding so that when our staffs are raised, they will speak without rancour.

Ajofia: Yes, plain language. An infant who pokes his tender fingers in a burning fire soon understands plain language, the hurtful difference between fascination and fear. Ajofia shudders as well for plain language. Because if the gods should descend from their lofty heights to engage mankind in plain talk, heads would burn and ears would sizzle like roast pork! But why waste words? The ear that will not harken is going with the head when cut off from the body.

Akaeze: Threats and curses shall pursue the enemies of Umudimkpa!

Chorus: Ise-e!

Akaeze: But genuine fears and concerns shall be conveyed to the king.

All: Long live the king!

Akaeze: Kingdom is people.

All: Kingdom is people.

Akaeze: What was the question about Umuachala?

Mmanko: It is for Okafor to answer since he was there and he is back now. Let us see his face and hear from his mouth.

Akaeze: Summon Okafor.

Echezo *[cupping his mouth with both hands, shouts]*: Okafor!

          [The shout is relayed off-stage. Enter Okafor.]

Dikeogu: Okafor, son of Odinagbo, where did you keep your eyes that the food in your hand turned mouldy?

Okafor: Revered high chiefs, fathers of the land, there is no eloquence in failure. But when something bigger than cricket blocks cricket's hole, the blame must sit elsewhere. A palm-wine tapper can never tell everything he witnessed from up-tree.

Dikeogu: Never mind, worthy fellow, that question had to be asked and that is why we asked it. The much we have seen with our own eyes, has any of us found a mouth to talk about it?

Ebekuo: Okafor, were you the only one they captured?

Okafor: I counted five others; but all were released before me.

Ebekuo: Were you tortured or put in danger at any time?

Okafor: Great fathers, these people were going to kill us all. The anger was like noon madness. It was Obiora's coming that saved us. It was no child's play.

Mmanko: How can we be sure they are not holding some of our people still? It is good to meet their demand but it is not wise to run a blind race from here to Umuachala.

Okafor: I cannot hide the truth from you, fathers though I had promised on oath to keep the silence. A son of the soil is still a hostage there. He took our place to break the deadlock.

Orimili: That kind of nobility is pure Umudimkpa. Who is the brave warrior?

Okafor: Your son, Obiora ... I warned him of the dangers, but he was adamant.

[Lights dim in the stunned silence. Ajofia's refrain refloats]

Ajofia's voice: Those who deprive the gods of their due sacrifice expose themselves as standby sacrifice. Ajofia will not mourn anyone that will not be warned . . . . The head that is used to break a coconut does not join the feast . . . . The place of honour for the loudest cockerel is the pot of soup . . . .

Orimili *[dazed and nervous, rises slowly]*: Akaeze, a brief word with you, please.

[Akaeze joins Orimili in a corner]

Ajofia's voice *[refloating]*: An infant who pokes his tender fingers in a burning fire soon understands plain language, the hurtful difference between fascination and fear . . . . . If the gods should descend from their lofty heights to engage mankind in plain talk, heads would burn and ears would sizzle like roast pork.

Orimili *[anxiously]*: Akaeze, this boy has put my feet out on the road. I have enemies in Umuachala.

Akaeze: Orimili, calm down.

Orimili: *[nervously]* I have no wish to contend with the gods.

Akaeze: Listen to me, Orimili.

Orimili: You heard Ajofia's repeated words. I have decided, Akaeze. I will vote their way. Seventy slave heads.

Akaeze: Hear me, Orimili. No amount of slave blood can change the purpose of the gods. Do not betray a son who has taught the whole kingdom how to be men.

Orimili: What is the use of all his outing if he is brought home a coffin? Akaeze, I'd rather have my son alive a coward than dead a hero.

Akaeze: Who says Obiora is dying? And if dying, is it this folly in blood that will save him? Let's stand fast today and confront the fear of tomorrow that holds us captive to yesterday. Your son,

Obiora has given a purpose to his life and a meaning to ours. A life invested in a worthy purpose does not die.

[Oyidi'a joins them in the corner]

Oyidi'a: You did not invite me, but I feel your pain, Orimili. If it is any comfort, my heart tells me that Obiora is safe. Still, I will rally the womenfolk on both sides to restrain you men from these frequent fights. Our children shall no longer be killed like rodents while we creep around and cry in the dark holes of custom.

[Lights brighten]

Orimili: Kingdom is people.

Akaeze & Oyidi'a: Kingdom is people.

Orimili *[intones and all join, taking up their staffs]*:

> *Ebunu mmili magbulu n'uwa*
> *K'anyi gaanu fu*   *Let's go and see*
> *Onye ebuna ya n'obi*   *Let none keep him in mind*
> *Onye ebenalu ya akwa*   *Let none grieve for him*
>
> *Ebunu mmili magbulu n'uwa*
> *K'anyi gaanu fu*   *Let's go and witness*
> *Onye ebuna ya n'obi*   *Let none keep him in mind*
> *Onye ebenalu ya akwa*   *let none grieve for him*

[Fade]

135

ACT 3, SCENE 6

Throne room at Umudimkpa palace, moments later same morning. The high chiefs and Oyidi'a are seated, listening. Ebekuo and Mmanko standing, interpret the coded broadcast of the council's decisions which the ekwe is playing.

Ebekuo: The king traveled
             The king traveled
             Long live the king

Mmanko: The king is mending, needs a rest
             See his chiefs
             Bother him not

Ebekuo: To Umuachala, salutations
             To Umuachala, peace
             Umuachala good days with us

Mmanko: There are two who never war
             Dimkpa and Achala, true brothers
             They are one and never war

Ebekuo: The king is back and all may cheer
             The free-born is free
             The numbered, safe.

Mmanko: The free-born is free
             The numbered are safe
             All may cheer, the king is back.

Akaeze: That man, Echezo beats *ekwe* like no man in the present age.

Ebekuo: I hardly can follow the fumbling notes we hear nowadays, but with Echezo it is different. His rendition is always precise.

Dikeogu: His father was great in his days too. A son following his father's footsteps is pure delight.

[Echezo bursts in]

Echezo: Akaeze! High chiefs! There is bad news! Bad news from Agbala shrine. It's a murder, there's been a murder. Akwamma is dead! Killed by her own son!

Oyidi'a: Ifediba?

[Enter Ifediba, flanked by Ebili and Chime. He is looking very dejected,
a half-empty calabash in hand.]

Ifediba: No, my brother Umunna killed her . . . And my friend, Apiti has fled, the brain behind this deed, and I am left in mourning to wonder who I am—slave or prince, bastard or orphan. I feel used and dumped, like an abused masquerade, but who can I blame for these things? If I had listened to the counsel of years, I would be seated on that throne. Instead, I kicked in blind haste the world at my feet. I followed Apiti, Slippery Mud that Spoils the Unwary, and he has led me to quicksands. A fellow who trades curses with his own father is not a guide to follow, I have found too late. Akaeze, it is your victory.

Akaeze: It was not a fight, young man. Kingdom is people.

All Chiefs: Kingdom is people.

Akaeze: You only owe me the snuff box that was passed to you in error. You must return it.

[Ifediba kneels before the chiefs]

137

Ifediba: I never thought a day would see me kneel like this, but humility is hardly a choice on the brink of humiliation. I plead, not for my life. It is a concluded tale of missed opportunities and wasted hopes; and the tragic path of misadventure laments the dignity of the road not taken. I plead only for Ajachi. Our lives are in your hands. Make me a prisoner, slave, outcast or whatever custom permits; but spare the life of this hapless wench and the child in her womb.

Akaeze: It is very unfortunate, young man, but the person whose name you called does not belong here.

Ifediba: You are elders and you have known the rush of passion and the heat of love. The baby in her womb is mine.

Akaeze: Candour is admirable but no cover for recklessness. Planting a seed when land ownership is not settled is a bad rush. It yields unpleasant fruits.

Ifediba: Our world is filled with heartaches and heart-breaks from treachery and deceit—men who deny seed and deed for the sake of appearances, women who cheat for fun or fortune, and children who are doomed to live their parents' lies. I hoped to make a difference in my personal case, standing by the woman who gave me her whole being.

Ajofia: Akaeze, we are wasting time! What business have we got with this rambling stranger?

Dikeogu: He should find us the missing snuff box! and not a replacement please!

Ebekuo: Let us be patient and hear from him what he expects from us.

Ajofia: In case no one has noticed, the gods have drawn first blood. Plain language!

138

Akaeze: Get up, young man. No one in this council is interested in your humiliation. But no one can help you either.

Ifediba: Then, help that poor girl, Ajachi. Save her from the fury of Umuachala. For the sake of the unborn baby.

Akaeze: It is too late. The person whose name you called is by now approaching her own country. The troops took her away with her family.

[Ifediba rises to his feet]

Ifediba: Talk is needless then . . . but I cannot walk away without a word of gratitude . . . to you, high mother. I feel you for ever; and you will always be special. Ebili, you kept faith alive, rushing back to stand by me this darkest moment of my life . . . . Have a mouthful of your favourite brew . . . you deserve the best, my man . . . . remember how we shared . . . the sweetest joy of manhood is boyhood remembered.

[He holds the base of the calabash as Ebili takes a huge gulp. They hug affectionately, then Ifediba moves away, fishing out a wrap from a pouch in his waist area. He waves it aloft to Chime]

Chime, only you and I know this secret. *[He empties it into the calabash and shakes it]* You will tell the high chiefs how close they rode to sunset this morning . . . And do this too, for me: tell our fellow youths out there, those who earnestly want to build for tomorrow, that they must seek wisdom from the mouth of elders for we were not there yesterday when they laid today's foundation. Tell them that for me . . .

[He drinks as Chime runs forward too late. Everyone is up. Chime wrestles the calabash from Ifediba who slowly slumps to his knees, clutching his stomach, coughing weakly]

Oyidi'a: What is it? What is it?

Akaeze: What is this one to be called?

Chime: Apiti wanted this for you but Ogbuagu stopped me from
           mixing it in the wine you drank this morning. Everyone of
           you would have died as he is dying now. It is the deadliest
           drug in the world.

                         [*All watch in horror as Ifediba writhes*]

Ebili: Son or stranger, there goes a great eagle
           A sower of love whose silo was for all
           He loathed wrongs that the settled ages have fruited
           And dreamt a plucking down to plant aright
           Fate has fouled; the mice of mischief messed
           But the twinkling stars above lament with me for ever
           The passing of a dream, a dawn that would not come . . . .

Chime: We, his friends shall set custom aside and give him a burial fit
           for a prince. Those who condemn him will fight us with the
           mad rage of tradition in their warped sense of duty. These are
           the pretenders, self-seekers and opportunists—masquerades
           who fill this world with strange seeds, denying in daylight
           their misdeeds of night. The custom of this age may mock
           true heroes and dress villains in undeserved honours. But
           the heavens will strip all things naked by and by.

Dikeogu [*to Orimili*]: Whose son is that one?

                         [Curtains]